Jentezen Franklin is a God-sized dreamer! His book *Believe That You Can* will inspire you to dream bigger than you've ever dreamed before and equip you to achieve everything God has planned for you.

—CRAIG GROESCHEL
SENIOR PASTOR, LIFECHURCH.TV
AUTHOR, *CHAZOWN*

There's something incredible about discovering your God-breathed dream and destiny, but more powerful still is pursuing it with your whole heart. Jentezen Franklin is a great friend, an inspiring teacher, and a fellow dreamer. His wisdom and experience gained in pursuit of the amazing call on his life will inspire you to realize the divinely implanted dream God has placed in you!

—BRIAN HOUSTON
SENIOR PASTOR, HILLSONG CHURCH

Jentezen does an exceptional job of revealing the riveting truth and severity of God-given dreams and the vital role they play in you fulfilling your destiny. Wherever you are in your journey, this book will empower you to embrace the process, keep climbing the mountain, and be reassured that He is building character, faith, and strength in you along the way. It's biblical, relational, and practical in its entirety and will impact you to the core.

—JOHN BEVERE
AUTHOR/SPEAKER
MESSENGER INTERNATIONAL

Nothing is more important, after you come to know Jesus Christ, than to get God's dream for your life. It's the reason you exist and your purpose for living. When you don't have it, you just drift around. It's only when you discover why God made you and what He wants you to do with your life that God makes sense. God shapes our dreams, and then they shape us.

—RICK WARREN
PASTOR, SADDLEBACK CHURCH
AUTHOR, *THE PURPOSE-DRIVEN LIFE*

If you need encouragement to keep your dreams alive, empowerment to bring your dreams to full fruition, or if you need to be reminded that God is faithful and you are not forgotten, then this book is for you. Prepare to be blessed, expect your life to change, and watch your God-given dreams come true while reading these anointed pages written by God's man and servant Jentezen Franklin.

—CECE WINANS
AWARD-WINNING GOSPEL RECORDING ARTIST

Believe That You Can

Believe That You Can

Jentezen Franklin

Charisma
HOUSE
A STRANG COMPANY

Most STRANG COMMUNICATIONS/CHARISMA HOUSE/CHRISTIAN LIFE/EXCEL BOOKS/FRONTLINE/REALMS/SILOAM products are available at special quantity discounts for bulk purchase for sales promotions, premiums, fund-raising, and educational needs. For details, write Strang Communications/Charisma House/Christian Life/Excel Books/ FrontLine/Realms/Siloam, 600 Rinehart Road, Lake Mary, Florida 32746, or telephone (407) 333-0600.

BELIEVE THAT YOU CAN by Jentezen Franklin
Published by Charisma House
A Strang Company
600 Rinehart Road
Lake Mary, Florida 32746
www.strangdirect.com

Unless otherwise noted, all Scripture quotations are from the King James Version of the Bible.

Scripture quotations marked NASU are from the New American Standard Bible—Updated Edition, Copyright © 1960, 1962, 1963, 1968, 1971, 1972, 1973, 1975, 1977, 1995 by The Lockman Foundation. Used by permission. (www.Lockman.org)

Scripture quotations marked NIV are from the Holy Bible, New International Version. Copyright © 1973, 1978, 1984, International Bible Society. Used by permission.

Scripture quotations marked NKJV are from the New King James Version of the Bible. Copyright © 1979, 1980, 1982 by Thomas Nelson, Inc., publishers. Used by permission.

Scripture quotations marked NLT are from the Holy Bible, New Living Translation, copyright © 1996. Used by permission of Tyndale House Publishers, Inc., Wheaton, IL 60189. All rights reserved.

Scripture quotations marked THE MESSAGE are from *The Message: The Bible in Contemporary English*, copyright © 1993, 1994, 1995, 1996, 2000, 2001, 2002. Used by permission of NavPress Publishing Group.

Design Director: Bill Johnson
Cover Designer: Justin Evans

Library of Congress Cataloging-in-Publication Data:

Franklin, Jentezen, 1962-
  Believe that you can / Jentzen Franklin. -- 1st ed.
     p. cm.
  Includes bibliographical references.
  ISBN 978-1-59979-348-1
  1. Dreams--Religious aspects--Christianity. 2. Visions. 3. Success--Religious aspects--Christianity. 4. Vocation--Christianity. I. Title.

  BR115.D74F73 2008
  248.4--dc22

                                          2008033596

First Edition

08 09 10 11 12 — 9 8 7 6 5 4 3 2
Printed in the United States of America

Contents

Acknowledgments | xiii

Introduction: Who's Been Dumping on Your Dream? | 1

1 **Write the Vision** | 9

Your dream is a very specific vision for a very specific outcome. Your dream is powerful because it comes from God. Write it down as soon as you can, and keep track of it.

2 **Discovering Your Mission in Life** | 23

Dreams that are from God go through a process of birth, death, and resurrection. Let the biblical story of Joseph remind you of the stages of the journey of your dream.

3 **You Will Come to Vision** | 43

A vision from God will stop you, send you, strengthen you, and stretch you. Keep standing on the revelation every step of the way. God will build your confidence the same way He helped Gideon see himself with new eyes.

4 Take Hold of Your Dream | 65

God will make sure you find your dream and destiny. The stages of discovery are: "I thought it. I caught it. I bought it. I sought it. I got it. I taught it!" Here is how to hang on tightly to it once you have it, lest doubts and fears loosen your hold on your dream.

5 Unfolding Your Dream | 75

Fulfilling your dream is an unfolding process. It may be fast or slow, and your initial passion and favor may give way to a time of testing and difficulty. Keep looking to God. He will bring you through to the fulfillment of your destiny.

6 Making Assets of Your Liabilities | 91

New strength will arise from your times of testing. Often your liabilities will become your assets as your weakness is converted into God's strength. Here is how to persevere past the limitations and hindrances that will come against you.

7 Living in the Faith Zone | 113

God will use your circumstances to keep you living in the "faith zone." He will show you how to break through every barrier. Learn three secrets to success from the Old Testament farmer Shamgar: start where you are; use what you have; do what you can.

8 Don't Let Go of Your Dream | 133

Caleb said, "That's my mountain," and he held on to his dream for forty years of wilderness wandering. Although he was realistic, he had no fear of the giants in the land, and he never wavered in his vision.

9 Keep Climbing | 153

To fulfill the vision God gives us for our lives, we have to break through old ways of thinking and acting. Be a mountain climber, not a camper or a quitter, and you will conquer your mountain!

10 Never Doubt Your Vision | 165

If God has His hand on your vision, you never need to second-guess it. Don't be discouraged or "despise small beginnings." He may need to adjust your assumptions and your motives, but with His help, you can learn the sure signs of a true vision from God.

11 Never Too Old | 183

You're never too old to dream. Consider all of the people who did not start following their dreams until they were old. Regardless of your circumstances, you can shoot your "arrows" of faith and praise and see amazing results.

12 Put Away Your Measuring Stick | 203

God created you for a high call. Do not ever put limits on what God can do. Believe you can fulfill His high call on your life. You can do it!

Notes | 219

Acknowledgments

I WANT TO EXTEND A SPECIAL THANK-YOU TO my precious wife, Cherise, and our five wonderful children. Because of your love and support, I believe that I can.

Thank you also to those who have labored to make this work possible: Richie Hughes, my staff, and the Charisma House team.

And finally, thank you to the faithful congregation of Free Chapel and all of the *Kingdom Connection* partners. All things are possible to those who believe.

WHO'S BEEN DUMPING ON YOUR DREAM?

I HEARD A STORY ABOUT A COUPLE IN Southern California who lived in the foothills of the mountains. One day as they were hiking through a canyon, they noticed wild mushrooms growing everywhere. They decided to pick the mushrooms and take

1

them home. They invited some friends over for a "mushroom party." No, they didn't smoke them; they cooked them. They sautéed the mushrooms, breaded them, and fried them. They made mushroom omelets, mushroom salad, and mushroom soup. They even concocted some mushroom desserts.

After dinner, as all of the guests were gathered at the table, having a great time, the host went into the kitchen with the leftovers. He had an old, lazy cat, so he decided to feed it with some scraps from the table. The cat gobbled up the mushrooms.

Some time later, the host went back into the kitchen and found the cat lying on the floor, foaming at the mouth and panting for breath. He immediately phoned the veterinarian, who advised the man that he and his dinner guests had better get to the emergency room as soon as possible to have their stomachs pumped. The vet suspected that they had picked poisoned toadstools instead of mushrooms.

After going to the hospital and having their stomachs pumped, the people finally made it back home. They made their way into the kitchen, expecting to see their cat lying lifeless on the floor. Instead, the cat was in the corner of the kitchen with a brand-new litter of kittens!

Imagine that! Have you ever felt like that? What they thought were death pains were, in reality, birth pains! It may look like your dream is foaming at the mouth and panting for its final breath, when in reality you're closer to giving birth to your dream than you've ever been.

If you are discouraged and feel as though your dream is dying, don't give up! Don't give up too soon on your dream. It may be you're just having birth pains, not death pains. It's always too soon to quit. When you've been through hell, what's five more yards?

Keep going. Keep dreaming the dream that God has put into your heart. If it were easy, anyone could do it.

It's always too soon to quit.

It can be the same with you and your life. You can misread the message of your circumstances and thereby miss your destiny. As you read this book, I want to equip you so that won't happen. I want to equip you to *believe that you can* reach your dream.

When you begin to pursue your dream, somebody will always emerge to try to steal it. Often it will be someone who never had a dream of their own, or if they did, they abandoned it. It could even be a family member who constantly reminds you of what God couldn't or wouldn't do through someone like you.

The question is not can you dream, but do you have the courage to act on it?

What do you dream about? What has God enabled you to see that does not yet exist? You will never outdream God! Listen: "God can do anything, you know—far more than you could ever imagine or guess or request in your wildest dreams!" (Eph. 3:20, THE MESSAGE).

God loves dreamers. He's the giver of new dreams and the mender of broken ones. When you dream, you move closer to the way He sees things. In that moment, you rise above your limitations; you move from where you are to where He wants you to be. In other words, you begin to see your goals in their completed state. The question is not can you dream, but do you have the courage to

3

act on it? Is there a dream in your heart? Has life buried it? Have others told you it's too late? Don't you believe it!

Pursue your dream no matter how far-fetched it may seem, for dreams are like children—they're your offspring. They're the joy of your present and the hope of your future. Protect them! Feed them! Encourage them to grow, because as long as you have a dream, you'll never be old! I'm talking about a God-given dream that leads to God-honoring results. God has a dream for you, and if you will seek Him, He will reveal it.

Your dreams usually won't arrive with the sound of blaring trumpets. You can miss them. They are very fragile. They tend to come very gently, and they may grow very slowly. Dreams are almost like a divine mist, and one harsh breath from some critic can dissolve it. All it takes is one negative word from a cynical person to crush a dream.

You need to be careful of dream assassins. Make sure you're not assassinating your own dream, because you may be your own worst critic. It's OK to talk *to* yourself, but not *at* yourself. Be careful not to talk yourself out of your dream. Instead, talk yourself *into* it. Believe that you can fulfill your dream, and you will!

Are you in a bad marriage? You can ask God to give you a vision for a healed marriage. Do you have money trouble? Dream for something better than being messed up financially for the rest of your life.

I use the words *dream* and *vision* interchangeably, and both of them are related to your destiny. The book you are holding will help you steer as you move along the journey of your dream. My dream is to help you unlock your dreams, and my prayer is that you will step out in faith to claim your destiny.

God is a dreamer too.

You are never more like God than when you're dreaming, because God is a dreamer from the beginning. His nature is in you, and that's why you can look at something that appears to be nothing going nowhere and believe in it. God makes things out of nothing, and He has passed on to you the ability to do the same thing—to make something out of what you cannot see. Faith is reaching up and grabbing hold of nothing and holding on until it becomes something. Dreaming things into existence is God's specialty. "It shall be even though it is not" is the very nature of the God who created you in His likeness.

He created you and me so that He could bring His kingdom to the world. He inspires and energizes our dreams so that He can accomplish what He wants to accomplish. He looks for people anywhere who will take seriously the dreams that He has placed in their hearts, believing that all things are truly possible with this God of the dream.

Be careful not to talk yourself out of your dream. Instead, talk yourself into it. Believe that you can fulfill your dream, and you will!

You may have a dream to become the greatest musician in the world, or to start your own business, or to become a professional athlete or a doctor or a lawyer. If the Holy Spirit has gifted you, and if you spend time with Him and He empowers you to practice and become skilled, you can do it. The important thing is to spend time with God, because when you spend time with Him, He unlocks your dreams and empowers you to walk them out.

Believe that you can.

I know this works, because I'm living it myself. At one time, all I had in my life was a dream. All I had was something inside of me. Around me I didn't have any parts of the dream yet, but something in me kept saying, "It's out there! It's out there! It's out there! Go after it. There's ministry out there."

When I was single, I had the dream of a beautiful wife. And today I have a dream wife; I really do. I don't know where I would be without my wife. I don't know what I would do without my wife. Cherise is beautiful inside and out. With her, God has given me dream children. They're beautiful. They're healthy and strong. They love God, and they want to do God's will. What more could a man ask for?

I remember almost two decades ago when the Lord called me to Gainesville, Georgia. When I drove into the city the first time, all I had was a dream. I had a dream that God would raise up a mighty church here that would be able to touch the nations for Him, where people would get saved, where deliverance would flow, and where people would be filled with God's precious Holy Spirit.

Now I'm standing right in the middle of the fulfillment of that dream. The church is growing so fast that anything I could write about it would be outdated by the time you read it. In my finances, I'm living a dream life. I have a beautiful home. Now I have blessings all around me. Sometimes I feel like saying, "Lord, I'm like those who dreamed." (I'm sure I must be the person Psalm 126:1 was written for.)

These days, I travel all over the world. I'm preaching in the nations of the world, preaching for my heroes, people whom I never dreamed I would meet, men and women of God whom I don't even feel worthy of being around. When I'm preaching, it's humbling to look down and see them sitting on the first row. I tell you, it's a "dream" life.

Once, I had a dream for a music ministry that would touch the world. Recently we signed a contract for a music project that's going all over the world. That's just one more part of this level of life where dreams are coming true, and all I can say is, "Is this really happening?"

God has blessed my life, and He's made it into a dream life. He wants to bless you with your dream life too—He really does.

Chapter 1

WRITE THE VISION

ONE DAY I WAS BROWSING THROUGH AN old notebook that was full of sermon notes that dated back more than fifteen years. While I was reading that notebook, I found a list of goals that I had listed for my church. I had included goals such as filling every seat in our balcony, starting our first twenty-one-day all-church January fast, and expanding our television ministry from one cable station to more stations.

Looking back, it was neat to see how God did so much more than I could have imagined when I wrote the list. Since that time, not only was the balcony filled, but we also built a larger facility—and filled it too—and now we are in the process of expanding our present sanctuary. The television ministry has expanded to three thousand stations on a number of national and international networks.

I had no idea when I jotted down these dream seeds and ideas that God would take our first twenty-one-day church fast and turn it into a national and international movement that would generate millions of hits on our Web site every year during our annual fast. Nor did I ever dream that a *New York Times* best-selling book on fasting would be produced from that simple goal that was inspired by the Holy Spirit and followed through by our congregation every year.

I'm hesitant to mention all of these blessings because I don't want to come across as a braggadocio. To the contrary, I know God deserves all the glory! But He uses ordinary people who believe that they can reach their God-given dreams.

Write It Down

A lot of people talk about having "vision" for their lives, but they don't understand the process or the journey of a vision. They say that God has given them a "dream" of something, but as time goes on, they lose track of it. They don't really know what a dream is supposed to look like.

---

*The enemy does not want you
to keep track of your vision. He
wants to distract you from it.*

I love what the verse says in the beginning of the second chapter of the Book of Habakkuk, because it highlights the purpose of a dream or vision, and it also gives some very practical advice on how to handle it:

> Then the LORD answered me and said:
> "Write the vision
> And make it plain on tablets,
> That he may run who reads it.
> For the vision is yet for an appointed time;
> But at the end it will speak, and it will not lie.
> Though it tarries, wait for it;
> Because it will surely come,
> It will not tarry....
> The just shall live by his faith."
>
> —HABAKKUK 2:2–4, NKJV

That's helpful. God is saying, "Write the vision." As soon as you grasp what your vision is, God wants you to write the vision down so that you can be focused on what He has revealed. He doesn't want you to lose track of it.

The enemy does *not* want you to keep track of your vision. He wants to distract you from it. He wants to substitute a different vision so that you become diverted and discouraged. But if you have it written down, you can remember what God spoke to your

11

heart, and you can go back to that point of reference and remind yourself, "This is what the Lord said." My Bible is marked from one end to the other with things that I've heard the Lord speak to me.

It's good to "make it plain," as the Lord said to Habakkuk, because if you don't make it plain, you won't know where you're going, and you'll be like the man who jumped on a horse and took off going in all directions. He ended up going in circles. Make it as plain as you can. The Lord's way is not complicated.

Beginning with a burden

Back at the very beginning of the Book of Habakkuk, we read this line: "The burden which the prophet Habakkuk saw" (Hab. 1:1). The *burden* (usually we think of a burden as something heavy to carry) was something he *saw* (we see with our eyes). I don't carry things with my eyes; do you? Isn't that an unusual way to put it? And yet it's not so odd when you think about it, because any vision from the Lord begins with just that—a *burden*. At first, God will place a burden on your heart.

What does a burden feel like? Habakkuk said three things about his burden. He said, "I felt it. I saw it. And I heard it." Something came over his heart, and he felt it. He saw a need, and God burdened him with it. After a while, God transferred it from being a burden to becoming a vision.

When it changed from a burden to a vision, it became plain. God showed it first to Habakkuk as something he could feel, like a burdensome weight, and then God said it outright. And you know what? God does not mumble. When God speaks, you don't have to say, "I wonder if I just heard Him." When He speaks, it's not "maybe" or "I hope so." When God speaks, a knowing comes into your spirit, and you have a definite sense. You'll think, "I have just heard from the Lord."

When it becomes plain like that to you, write it down.

Do not be one of those people who go through life and never have a vision. It is a terrible thing to never, ever catch a glimpse of what God has for your life. Scripture says, "Eye hath not seen, nor ear heard, neither have entered into the heart of man, the things which God hath prepared for them that love him. But God hath revealed them unto us by his Spirit: for the Spirit searcheth all things, yea, the deep things of God" (1 Cor. 2:9–10).

So, in a way, we have no excuse except ignorance for not knowing God's vision for our lives, because God *always* has something for each one of us.

The way to find out what He has for you is to get alone with Him. Spend time with Him. Make it possible for Him to take you up a little bit higher so that He can begin to slip a burden into your heart and put a vision before the eyes of your spirit.

Keeping your focus

Besides giving you a vision in the first place, God wants you to focus on Him as you walk it out, because you are going to need His strength to do it. Without His strength along the way, you will not be able to accomplish what God has given you.

A vision is a supernatural thing, and you need to walk it out with supernatural power. That's the same as living by faith, as Habakkuk put it at the end of that passage I quoted at the beginning of this chapter. If you don't keep your focus on God and on what He has told you, and if you don't keep walking by faith the whole time, you stand a very good chance of losing track of your vision.

It is important to keep your focus not only on God but also on the vision itself. Paul said, "This one thing I do" (Phil. 3:13). He did not say, "These forty things I dabble in." Get a clear idea of what God wants you to do, and get focused on it. Then, hold on and run with it. You may pant with desperation sometimes, but don't give up. You are like a bulldog with a bone.

You are going to need that kind of focused determination in order to keep going when the going gets rough. Paul had a vision that showed him he was supposed to go to Macedonia. It was exciting, the birth of the vision. But when he got there, they beat the daylights out of him and threw him into prison. That could have been the death of his vision right there, but then an angel came and set him free to fulfill the vision. In essence, the angel resurrected his vision. That's the journey a vision will take you through every time—birth, death, and resurrection.

One of the most important ways you can tell if a dream or a vision is from God is that it will always be bigger than you are.

When people come up to me all giddy and say, "Oh, Jentezen, God has given me a vision. I'm going to do this and do that," they don't understand that it's going to get difficult at some point. Of course, it's great if they're excited about their vision—they're going to need all that energy later!

It is bigger than you.

One of the most important ways you can tell if a dream or a vision is from God is that it will always be bigger than you are, and it will always be bigger (and better) than you think.

A vision from God is orchestrated by God Himself. He is always working behind the scenes, pulling things together and making things come out right. He is preparing other people, people you never met before, people you never dreamed of, so that they are ready to catch what you're going to throw and throw what you're going to catch. You may think, "Here I have a vision from God. Now it's all up to me to make it happen." But it's really *His* vision. It's up to Him to make it happen.

All you have to do is obey step by step. Your vision will happen as God moves you and, simultaneously, as He moves other people and circumstances. All of these kingdom connections will start to occur. They'll come from every direction. That's not coincidental; it's God.

How is it connected to the harvest?

Not only should you expect your vision from God to be big, but you should also look for how it is connected to the harvest of His kingdom. Joseph had a dream about being in a harvest field (Gen. 37). The harvest portion of your dream may not be quite as obvious to you as it was to him, but look for the connections. How is *your* dream connected to the harvest?

The word *harvest* represents souls being brought into the kingdom of heaven. *Harvest* means building God's kingdom, building the local church, and increasing the influence of God's kingdom in the world around you.

You may have said, "I want to make a million dollars in my business." If you can connect that dream to the harvest, then God can bless it. (For example: "I'll use my resources to support my local church.") You may have said, "I want to be a star athlete, and I want to play in professional sports." If you can tie your dream back to the harvest ("God, if You bless me and put me before thousands of people, I'll use my influence for the kingdom"), then He can bless it.

When you come to understand visions and dreams, it's not just a matter of getting what you want, which would be a selfish thing. God won't be committed to that. It's a matter of looking for the *harvest* connection. You see, a God-given dream always has a kingdom purpose.

Because God's ultimate purpose is to bring in the harvest, you and I need to dream harvest dreams. It's OK to dream of having a better house, a nicer car, a higher standard of living. That's fine. But at some point, instead of just saying, "Bless me," we need to be able to say, "Lord, use me. Help me fulfill my dream so I can be a blessing to others in Your kingdom."

God's dreams *will* come to pass.

Remember what the Lord said to Habakkuk? "For the vision is yet for an appointed time; but at the end it shall speak, and not lie: though it tarry, wait for it; because it will surely come, it will not tarry" (Hab. 2:3). In other words, even though your dream may seem slow to come about, you can depend on the fact that if a dream comes from God, it will always happen eventually.

A God-given dream always
has a kingdom purpose.

You may need to "wait for it" (Habakkuk's words). You may need patience and perseverance. But your patience will be rewarded, because it *will* come to pass.

When your initial excitement wears off and everything seems to have stalled, don't be surprised. This is normal. Every person goes through this. There is going to come a time when everything looks like the opposite of what you thought God told you. When it comes (and this may happen more than once), don't give up, don't cave in, don't throw in the towel. Though it tarries, though it lingers, though you're discouraged, though it seems as if the doors aren't opening and the money's not coming in and nothing is going right—wait for it. It *will surely* come to pass.

God's visions become reality. God's dreams happen. He may need to go find another dreamer (if you give up), but His *dream* will happen. You need to stick around long enough to see it happen. You have to be tenacious about your vision. You may have to go through as much opposition as a halfback running through a group of seven-foot-tall linebackers, but just grab that vision like a football and say, "I know I've got a word from the Lord, and here I go!" Take off running with it, hold it close to your chest, and don't stop.

One translation of that passage includes the words "panting with desperation." That's what happens when you can see the goal line up there and you're determined to give it all you have. People are trying to trip you up and yank that vision out of your arms, but

17

you just throw yourself forward, panting with desperation. You're desperate because you feel like you're running for your life. You just *have* to make it. And you will.

Response leads to results.

God will never give you the whole thing worked out ahead of time. He just tells you, "Go. I will fill in the details." You have to respond to that somehow. Ideally, you will respond immediately and obediently. God is looking for a spontaneous response from you when He tells you to do something. He doesn't want you to send it off to a committee for a thorough evaluation. He doesn't want you to take it too lightly, to forget about it, or to put it on a shelf. He wants you to do something right away.

The reason so many people are "stuck" where they are and they never go anywhere is that whenever God has told them to do something, they have pulled out their long list of questions before responding in faith. They say, "How can I afford it?" or "I'm too uneducated." If you wait until every question has been answered before you move, you'll never do anything. You'll never be more than 80 percent sure. If you are waiting to reach 100 percent sure, you will be paralyzed before you get there—it's called the "paralysis of analysis."

You may not know how something can ever happen, but when God says "Do this!" there's something about an immediate response that impresses Him. The rest of your response involves stepping out and walking by faith. Abraham didn't know how it would be possible to fulfill the vision God gave him. God had told him to get out of where he had been living and to go to a new place, some-place he didn't know yet, and God said that when he got there, He would tell him what to do next. Abraham was happily settled and well respected where he was. It seemed as if he had already accomplished his purpose in life. When God told him to go to a new place, Abraham could have raised all sorts of objections and questions, but, instead, he just went ahead and did what God had told him to do. That's impressive, and God wants each one of us to keep Abraham's example in mind.

If you wait until every question has been answered before you move, you'll never do anything.

When God calls you to do something, you have to be willing to go someplace new. Responding to God is going to mean *change* in your life. Did you know that change is a sure sign of God? The truth is that walking with God requires an ongoing, ever-changing experience. One of the sure signs that God is doing something in your life is that *change* is involved. One of the signs that God is preparing you for miracles is change.

Now, most of us are not too fond of change. In fact, we hate it. We go into change kicking and screaming. We prefer our old, familiar landscape and our customary routines. Maybe—just maybe—we become willing to step into something new once we have satisfied ourselves that we know what to expect and if we have worked out all the details ahead of time. But that's not how God works. He just puts you out there in some wilderness, and He makes sure that the only thing you have to hang on to is Him.

God will supply you with the next step as if He is giving you pieces to a puzzle. If you find the place where one piece fits and step forward, He will hand you another one. If you move when He says move, the details will fit themselves in.

Living in two states at one time

Just when you think you have your whole life figured out, God will come along and change everything. When I was forty-five years old, I had been pastoring in Gainesville, Georgia, for almost twenty years along with my wife and our five children. I was minding my own business, doing what God had called me to do, when suddenly change came knocking on my door.

In the summer of 2007 I was invited to Southern California to be on a national television program to promote my book *Right People, Right Place, Right Plan: Discerning the Voice of God.* After the program was taped, a pastor friend invited me to dinner. As we were riding on the interstate through Orange County, I noticed a church out of the corner of my eye. I inquired as to whose church it was. My pastor friend told me the name of the pastor. I was shocked because the pastor had called me the week before to inform me that he would be retiring from the church and relocating to the eastern part of the United States, and he would like to get together.

As my friend and I pulled into the parking lot of this 88,000 square-foot building right in the heart of Orange County, I couldn't help but be impressed with the pastor's dream. He had left his family, friends, and successful church to travel all the way across the nation to Southern California because God had given him a dream to build a church in Orange County. With very limited resources, he had managed to secure this large building in one of the most desirable locations in Orange County.

It was ten o'clock at night when we arrived. A man had come to let us in, and his sixteen-year-old son was with him. His son recognized me from TV, and they let us walk through the building. It just so happened that the sixteen-year-old, who walked through the building with us, had been fasting and praying for three days that God would send the right pastor to replace the retiring pastor. As I walked through the facility, I sensed that God had a very special plan for this church.

Just when you think you have your whole life figured out, God will come along and change everything.

So, I called the pastor who was retiring, and I started to tell him how amazed I was about what God had accomplished through his obedience. He began to weep over the phone. He told me that he felt impressed to encourage me to consider becoming the pastor of the church. I was stunned and excited at the possibilities.

After weeks of fasting and prayer, I agreed to pastor the church, with the unanimous consent of my wife and our five children. It sounds crazy, right? How can a pastor in Georgia also pastor a church in Southern California? If God tells you to do it, and you know He's called you, He'll make a way. Now, almost every Sunday after our services in Georgia, I board a plane with my family and fly to California in time for the 6:00 p.m. service in Orange County. The church has exploded in growth. Hundreds have been born again in the first few months. The sanctuary is already at capacity. We're seeing a mighty move of God in Orange County. The staff we've needed and the resources we've needed have fallen into place as we simply stepped out in faith and did what God told us to do.

It required massive change on our part. Our lives have been changed by this new calling. The kids' schooling has been changed, and my schedule and travels have been radically altered. How long has it been since you were close enough to God for Him to disturb your schedule and routine? Are you up for the challenge of change? The fulfillment of your destiny lies on the other side of change.

REVIEW

Write the Vision

- Your dream will begin with a burden of some sort, and that burden will become a vision.

- You'll know your dream is from God if it is *bigger than you* and if it has to do with the *harvest* field of the kingdom of God.

- Keep a record of your dream so that you don't forget it. Write it down.

- God's dream *will* come to pass. Although it may seem to die for a time, God will resurrect it.

Chapter 2

DISCOVERING YOUR
MISSION IN LIFE

ONE WINTER DAY IN BILOXI, MISSIS-

sippi, a twenty-five-year-old woman

decided to kill herself. She couldn't take it anymore and

she wanted her life to be over. She went to a bridge over

the Mississippi River.

The water was frigid, and the bridge was high. She climbed over the railing and threw herself over. She hit the water with a terrible smack and started sinking.

Unbeknownst to her, a man on the bank of the river saw her jump. When he did not see her surface, he jumped in to rescue her.

She was sinking deeper when she heard him dive in. And then she started to hear this poor man flailing around. When he had jumped in, he had forgotten that he didn't know how to swim! This heroic idiot was splashing and screaming, "Help! Help!" so the woman who was trying to kill herself swam to him and pulled him out onto the bank. He was choking, so she gave him mouth-to-mouth resuscitation. Somebody called 911, and both of them were taken to the hospital. Both of them survived.

I read about this in a news article, and the journalist who wrote up the story ended it with these words: "That night, it wasn't the man who saved her life. It was *purpose* that saved her life." Her purpose was to save the drowning man. Instantly, she had a mission. And having a mission saved her own life.

What Is Your Assignment in Life?

The purpose of life is to live a life of purpose. God is looking for people to whom He can transfer His passion and dream. Israel's greatest enemies were not the giants without but the voices within—that voice on the inside that said, "It can't be done. Play it safe." If you're going to be a dreamer, God wants you to take risks! If you dream, it means you expose yourself to ridicule and failure. You can't pursue a dream without someone saying, "Who does he think he is?"

Negative speaking and thinking will keep you from God's best.

If you can't remember the last time you were criticized for something, chances are you're not doing anything. Don't be so fearful of what people might say about you that you abandon your God-given dream. Get a belly full of fire, passion, and enthusiasm, and seize the opportunities God sends your way. Believe that you can do all things through Christ who strengthens you.

The birth, death, and resurrection of your vision

When you first respond to God as I described in the previous chapter, you are bringing about the *birth* of your vision. And like everything else in the kingdom of God, a birth is followed by a *death*, and then by a *resurrection*.

The purpose of life is to
live a life of purpose.

Every one of God's visions and dreams goes through this process of birth, death, and resurrection. You have not really received a dream from God unless you've carried a burden, gotten all excited because you have given birth to a newborn vision, and then, often with great dismay, watched what seems to be a death. The vision dies—people leave; the money dries up; the situation goes haywire; you just can't figure out what to do about it.

Then, and only then, God will come through with a resurrection. He uses that process to sanctify that dream so that when it really does come to pass, it will not be an egotistical thing for you. Instead, you will be able to stand back and declare, "God did it! I almost gave up on it. I doubted the vision, but the Lord did it anyway!" You will know beyond a shadow of a doubt that God did it, because it used to look so hopeless. See, it really was bigger than you were. You really could not have brought that thing back to life like that. God broke the limits off. He raised it back up. He finished what He started.

I guarantee you—if you have a dream, the way you will know it's from God is if you see these three stages: the birth of the vision, the death of the vision, and the resurrection of the vision. If you are in the middle of that process right now, don't give up! The resurrection is coming. Just because your marriage seems to be on the rocks, don't give up on it. Just because your business is floundering, don't quit yet. Whether it's your marriage or business or anything else, ask the Lord to send you some encouragement and a new supply of faith. Hold on; help is coming.

Patience wins the race.

You have to endure patiently. Do you remember what the author of the letter to the Hebrews wrote? He exhorted the Hebrews with these words: "Let us run with patience the race that is set before us, looking unto Jesus the author and finisher of our faith" (Heb. 12:1–2).

In other words, it might take a long time, but victory is achievable. It's like the torch race in the ancient Greek Olympics that was different from other races. In the other races, the winner was the one who crossed the finish line first. But in the torch race, they lit a bunch of torches and handed them out to every runner. They started the race with the fires burning, and the only way you could win the torch race was to finish with your fire still lit. Just because you made it first didn't count until they checked to see if your fire was still burning.

The race was not to the swift (Eccles. 9:11). Sometimes the winner would be the one who looked like he was barely making it. Only by patient persistence and by letting others pass him could the victor claim his prize. Everyone else might seem to outrun him and outdo him, but *they wouldn't win if they lost their fire.*

See what I mean? I want to be like a winning torch racer. I want to keep moving as fast as I can, but I am not going to lose my fire if I can help it. The important thing is not how quickly I can make it, how quickly my church or my ministry grows, how fast my business grows, how many records I break—it's whether or not I still have the fire of God burning when I cross the finish line. Am I willing to stay around not only for the birth of my vision but also for its death and the resurrection, which might take years?

Am I willing to be like my favorite animal on the ark—the snail? Only by persistence did he make it onto the ark, but he made it, and that's all that counted!

The Power of an Unforgettable Dream

Let me tell you about the unforgettable dream. I got the idea of an unforgettable dream from Moses, because even though he always had the dream of taking the people of Israel into the Promised Land, when he got to the end of his life and he could see the Promised Land from Mount Nebo, God said to him, "Moses, you're not going in." But Moses's dream was an unforgettable dream, and it stayed alive even when he died.

Many people would say, "He didn't make it." But that's not true, because when you look in the Book of Matthew, when Jesus was on the Mount of Transfiguration—*which was in the Promised Land*—Moses and Elijah came down out of heaven, and the

Bible says that they appeared on top of that mountain (Matt. 17:3). Moses got there! Moses's dream came to pass after all. His dream was to stand in the Promised Land. It took fifteen hundred years, but it *did* come to pass. That is a powerful, unforgettable dream!

The power of an unforgettable dream is that it just keeps going until, one of these days, it is fulfilled. It doesn't matter how many setbacks occur or how many obstacles are thrown in the way. It's never too late. It came from God, and it still belongs to Him. God made the promise, and He has the power to fulfill it.

It's never too late.

One of my favorite scriptures in the Bible is Amos 3:12, which says, "A shepherd who tries to rescue a sheep from a lion's mouth will recover only two legs or a piece of an ear. So it will be for the Israelites in Samaria" (NLT).

This paints a picture: the lion had devoured the lamb, leaving only a leg or two and a piece of an ear. The lion is Satan, who prowls around, "seeking someone to devour" (1 Pet. 5:8, NASU), and Satan devours the sheep, who represent the people of God.

The scripture says that when the shepherd saw that there was nothing left of that sheep except an ear and a couple of legs, remarkably, he walks over and snatches the ear and the legs from the mouth of the lion. Why? If I were the shepherd, I wouldn't do that. I would see that it's over. My sheep has been devoured. It's finished.

But the shepherd—who is a picture of Jesus—saw in that sheep something that was still redeemable. As long as you have an ear to hear and a leg to stand on (in other words, you're standing on what you've heard), it doesn't matter what the enemy has devoured. God can redeem it. It's not in what you've lost; it's in what you have left.

As long as you can hear and as long as you can hobble, you may stumble into your destiny; you may stagger into your dream. But if you have an unforgettable dream, you can stand on what you've heard God say, and He'll bring it to pass.

Does it seem as if the enemy has devoured your dream? Does it seem to be too late now?

It's never too late. We serve a God of resurrection, and He will resurrect your dream so that you can reach its fulfillment. As long as you still have an *ear* to hear, even as you're reading this book, He will be speaking to you. Then you can stand on what you've heard.

Nothing is impossible. Believe that you can!

Joseph and You

The story of Joseph is a perfect illustration of what this book is about—the power of a dream. In the story, the dreamer is Joseph, and he persisted for *years* through all kinds of difficulties. For a long time, his dream seemed to have died. He went through all sorts of things. But God kept his dream alive, and He resurrected it. In the end, Joseph's original dream was completely fulfilled.

Joseph, who had a couple of very specific dreams at the age of seventeen, went from being a favorite son in his father's home to being an *un*favored slave in a foreign land. When his envious brothers saw him coming, they said, "Behold, this dreamer cometh" (Gen. 37:19). They didn't even use his name, Joseph; instead, they just called him "this dreamer."

After becoming a slave in Egypt, he was in prison at one point. Then he was raised up to become the ruler over everything that the pharaoh of Egypt owned. That's when his brothers turned up again, and his dreams came to pass. (The story is in the Book of Genesis, beginning with chapter 37.)

You might think that this story is light-years away from your personal experiences in the twenty-first century. But you know what? You and I probably will have to pass the same tests as Joseph did before our dreams will come true. Let's draw out the main steps in the process.

Obtaining favor

Before you can step forward to claim the dream God is giving to you, you need to understand what "favor" is. Favor means that God has already prepared things ahead of you so that when you get there, you will walk into them. Favor is the way He makes "all things work together for good" (Rom. 8:28). Favor means that God has "centergized" everything on you. It means God has called you to the front of the line.

Joseph had favor, and everybody knew about it. His coat of many colors represented the favor of his father. He wore it proudly. That coat stood out! It wasn't brown or gray or beige. That coat was *loud*. It was so bright that it was almost psychedelic. It advertised favor.

It's the same with you and me. When God blesses you real good, it can be hard to conceal it. You aren't intentionally flaunting His favor in front of people, but people see it anyway. When God starts blessing you, He blesses you so that you will be seen by others as someone who is highly favored of God. He doesn't want you to be ashamed of His blessing. He doesn't want you to apologize for it.

Joseph's father put that coat on his son to prepare him for his dream. Anytime God begins to favor you and to bless you, it's to prepare you for a dream.

We enjoy a degree of favor from the moment we're saved, but in order to walk into the rest of our destiny, we need to receive more of it. The way it usually works in the kingdom of God is that you have to *ask* for favor. Words are powerful. God created the world by speaking words. If you don't open your mouth to declare that you want your purposes to line up with God's purposes, and if you don't ask for God's help, you won't receive it. "Ye have not," James said, "because ye ask not" (James 4:2).

When you open your mouth and ask for favor, God will rain it down on you. Ask the Lord for rain in the time of the latter rain. His favor is like a cloud of the latter rain. (See Zechariah 10:1; Proverbs 16:15.) So don't put it off! Raise your voice, and establish the fact that you are on the favor-receiving end right this minute, even if you just lost your job and you don't know where the next one is coming from.

Declare something like this: "I am highly favored of the Lord. His favor is making me irresistible. His favor is preceding me and making a way for me. He is making others look at me with favor. God has decreed it, and He has already sent it. It's like a cloud over me, and I'm just going to announce it. All I have to do is ask, and then I'll get in on the outpouring of favor."

Be sure to notice the connection between *fields* and favor. Joseph's favored status enabled him to believe his dream about a field with the sheaves of grain bowing down to his sheaf (Gen. 37:5–6). We can find another biblical example of the connection between fields and favor in the story of Ruth. Ruth made a specific request that she would be able to work in the *field* of someone who would show her favor (Ruth 2:2).

You have a field with favor in it too. Your field may not happen to have barley growing in it, but you do have a field. You can compare the harvest field of Joseph's dream and the harvest field of Boaz, where Naomi gleaned, to your own career "field." You may feel that you are supposed to go into the field of medicine or the field of teaching. If you pray before you set foot on your field and you pray to be led to the field of God's choosing, you will receive favor in your harvest field. Just open your mouth and ask.

Incidentally, Ruth shows us something else about how to be positioned for favor, and that is the importance of hanging around other people who carry favor. In her case, it was her mother-in-law, Naomi, who had been born in Bethlehem and who was one of God's chosen people. Ruth had come from Moab. The people of Moab were the opposite of chosen. In fact, they were cursed. But when Ruth decided to stick with Naomi, she started to walk into favor.

You can find favor that way too. When you look for a church, look for one that has the favor of God on it. When you get under leadership, look for leadership that has the favor of God on it. You won't be able to go any higher than the favor you're under. If you hang around people who have God's favor on them already, and then if you ask God to guide you to the field of His choosing for your life, you will be able to experience God's faithfulness firsthand.

In Ruth's case, Boaz noticed her, and the next thing you know, he married her. She went from picking up handfuls of barley to owning the whole plantation, all because she opened her mouth and asked for favor.

Dreaming of harvest

Notice again the setting of Joseph's first dream. It was a harvest field, where the grain was in the process of being harvested and bound into sheaves. I want to reemphasize the idea that your own field needs to be *connected to harvest*. You make your dream into a harvest dream when you make a vow to God that says, "Lord, if You bless this dream, I will use the influence to reach souls for You."

In Joseph's harvest dream, the harvested sheaves were bowing down to his sheaf. That doesn't mean that this was a selfish, prideful dream. In essence, the dream showed that wherever Joseph went, the full harvest would be reaped, and it would come under God's authority. Joseph had a role to play in the harvest, and then the harvest would bow down. The Bible says, "Every knee shall bow" (Isa. 45:23; Rom. 14:11).

So, if you have a dream, you can be sure that it's from God if it has something to do with the harvest. If you get a dream in your heart to change the school system, or to help open up your nation for revival, or to reap the people of your community into the kingdom by the thousands, then watch God carry that dream through to fulfillment. Those are harvest dreams!

Joseph didn't stop with one harvest dream. He dreamed another dream, and this time it was the sun and moon and stars that were bowing down. This dream was bigger and better than the first one. God's dreams are progressive, you know. Stop thinking that your best days are behind you. Your dream is ahead of you, and it is pointing you forward. It's bigger and better than anything that has happened in your past.

Stripped and put down

Of course, inevitably, if you are walking around displaying God's favor, and if, like Joseph, you happen to tell somebody about the full magnitude of your dream, you will be put down. (I've learned that some people want you to do good, but they just don't want you to do too good!)

People will get jealous, as Joseph's big brothers did, and they will strip you of your "special son" status. They will even throw you into a "pit."

Like Joseph's brothers, people will say, "Behold, here comes that dreamer." If you go with the dream God has given you, people will begin to see the dream that God has placed in your heart instead of seeing you. To them, it will seem bigger than your name. They may heap scorn on your dream too. One of the reasons they do that is because they can tell that the dream is going to come to pass. They're afraid of your dream. People don't bother to disparage someone else if they don't think the person's dream is powerful.

So if you have a lot of pressure on you right now and you seem to be seeing more adversity than blessing, I want to tell you that this is not an indication that you should give up. It very well could be an indication that the enemy knows you're closer to having your dream come to pass than you ever have been before. The enemy knows that he needs to conspire against you and attack you and stop you because your dream is for real. You can't quit now!

The fact is, if God placed that dream in your heart, and if you don't let go of it, nobody can stop it, not even the devil himself. Nobody's "no" can compete with God's "yes." If God says yes, then it's "yes and amen." If God opens a door, no man can shut it. What heaven hatches, hell cannot stop.

So what if people leave you? So what if they say they don't believe you or if they say that God is not with you? Your dream is still intact and moving forward. This is just a test you will have to pass before you get to the fulfillment of it.

So what if you get stripped of the outward expression of blessing and favor as Joseph got stripped of his special coat? So what if, in essence, people throw you in a pit? The inward expression of blessing is still there, even though it may be dry as a desert in the pit. It may have been a well or a cistern at one time, but now there's no water in it. There's no refreshing, but that is part of the test. When there's no external sign of blessing and no internal sense of blessing, your dream is being tested.

I've heard it said, "The test comes to teach you a lesson." But I never took tests in school to learn my lessons. The teacher would first teach me something and then give me a test. If God is putting you through a test, it is not because He wants to teach you something. It's a sign that He has already taught you something and now you're ready to get through the test.

Remember, the teacher is always silent during the test. Also remember that it's an open-book test! Open God's instruction book called the Bible, and read the instructions. Don't do it the way I did one Christmas, when I stayed up late trying to put a toy together. I thought I'd bypass reading the instructions because I thought I could figure it out by myself. After an hour of frustration, I finally found the instruction booklet, which actually began with these words: "When all else fails, read the instructions."

Maybe your dream is being severely tested and you're trying desperately to put all the pieces together. God's word to you today is this: Get back into the Word of God. Read the Word, and the Word will begin to read you! When you can't hear God, read God.

If you'll read God, you'll start hearing God again. When all else fails, read the instructions.

You already know what to do, even if you have been stripped on the outside and you're dry on the inside. Just stand there. And when you've done all, stand some more! Read the sixth chapter of Ephesians to remind yourself of the truth.

Later in the story of Joseph, he has two sons, and he names them Manasseh and Ephraim. *Manasseh* means "making forgetful," and *Ephraim* means "fruitfulness." Before you can walk all the way to the fulfillment of your dream, you need to have both forgetfulness and fruitfulness. Your past will come up to haunt you, and you will need to tell it, "Past, shut up!" You purposely forget about it. Then you can become fruitful.

The return of favor

If you wait long enough, favor will return. After Joseph's brothers had stripped off his coat of favor, they decided not to kill him but instead to sell him as a slave. And where did he end up? In the household of Potiphar, the chief bodyguard of the pharaoh of Egypt. That's not what Joseph's brothers had anticipated.

Even though Joseph was still just a teenager with no experience or training, everything that young man did prospered. It was as if he were wearing his coat of favor again, even though now he was dressed in Egyptian clothes. I think his way of walking must have been different from the other slaves. I think that even though he didn't have any distinguishing clothes or features, he had something on the inside that made him walk with his head up just a little bit higher, with his chest poked out just a little bit more, with a healthy disregard for the fact that he was being held captive as a slave.

It will be the same with you. The coat may be missing, but that is a temporary situation. In spite of what you haven't yet received, you are still blessed. It's just a matter of time. Just stand fast—even if you get thrown down again, which is what happened to Joseph. (See Genesis 39:19–20.)

Dream on.

I don't need to tell you that being thrown into prison was not part of Joseph's dream plan. He was in a dungeon with a bunch of people who were worse than slaves and were not going anywhere. You would think that this would have killed Joseph's dream once and for all. In prison, everyone's dreams seemed to be dead, except the dreams of the pharaoh's butler and the pharaoh's baker, each of whom had a literal dream, followed by the important dreams of Pharaoh himself.

There's an important lesson to remember here. Nobody had a dream in Egypt until Joseph the dreamer showed up, and then others began to have dreams about the harvest. If you want to have a God-given dream, you need to get around other dreamers. Dreamers inspire dreams in other people. Joseph's dream is what inspired the butler, the baker, and the pharaoh. When they got around him, their dreams began to manifest.

Are the people you're in relationship with inspiring your dream? Does the church you attend build your faith and cause your dream to kick? When Elizabeth came in contact with Mary, the baby began to leap in her womb (Luke 1:41).

Who is your pharaoh? Who is your baker? Who is your butler?

Who is your pharaoh? Who is the one whose dreams will include you and will promote you and then will finance your dream?

If you want to have a God-given dream,
you need to get around other dreamers.
Dreamers inspire dreams in other people.

And who will help you bring things together first so that you can get to that point? When you are walking out your destiny, two of the kinds of people who need to come into your life are the "bakers" and the "butlers." Who is your baker, and who is your butler? A baker is somebody who pulls it all together. A butler is somebody who opens doors for people.

A baker can take different ingredients—a handful of flour, an egg, and a pinch of salt—and make something out of it. He pulls things together and makes something. Many of us need the help of a "baker" to help us pull things together in our lives. Why won't that business come together? Why won't that marriage work better? You may need somebody who mentors you in how to pull it all together.

Then there is the butler, the door opener. He's somebody who's in the right place at the right time for you. He seems to appear from nowhere to open that door for you, and he often disappears after he does it. He gives you a door you can walk through, an opportunity. The butler turned out to be the one who got Joseph released from prison.

I remember a particular door opener in the history of our church. Free Chapel had started out in a former skating rink, and from there the church had moved into a little cinder-block building that would hold about fifty people. In 1975, the church once again relocated to a building on Browns Bridge Road in Gainesville,

Georgia. Hundreds of people began to come; we were growing fast. The church was growing so fast that by 1992 we had to move again to our fourth location on McEver Road in Gainesville.

One Saturday night, the respected evangelist R. W. Schambach gave me a phone call. He said he was in the area and that he'd like to preach the following night at my church. I had never met him in my life. Of course, I said, "Yes, you can preach at my church."

On Sunday night, he came in about twenty minutes late, which meant that I didn't get to talk to him at all before the service. He came up behind me as I was taking the offering and he asked me, "Can I obey the Lord?"

What do you say to R. W. Schambach when he asks you that? I said, "Sure, go ahead."

He took the microphone, and he spoke: "The Lord sent me here, and the Lord impressed me that this church is supposed to have a television ministry." Now, never in my wildest dreams had I expected that. And then he said to the people (who had just given one offering, remember), "Bring your offering." And people started bringing up thousands of dollars. Within a few minutes, $138,000 had been raised.

We went out the next week and bought three television cameras and our editing suite. We started out on one tiny TV station in Athens, Georgia. One thing after another happened (more butlers opened more doors!) and before we knew it, we were preaching to millions of people. I had no idea it could happen so fast. Without me pulling any strings, it fulfilled the dream I had preached to my people more than once in our Browns Bridge Road sanctuary. I remember getting up in that pulpit when we really didn't have any money or a whole lot of people and saying, "One day we shall preach the gospel to the world from the red clay hills of northeast Georgia!"

R. W. Schambach was a "butler" for my dream. He just showed up and opened the right door—and it was a big one! God has butlers, bakers, and pharaohs assigned to your dream. Begin to ask Him to release them in your life.

Fulfillment at last

We all know how Joseph's story ends. You can read the rest of it in Genesis 42–46; it's one of the best stories in the Bible. Pharaoh released Joseph and promoted him to prime minister. The famine was so widespread that it drove Joseph's brothers out of Canaan and caused them to come in supplication before their own brother. They ended up bowing before him, just as those sheaves had done in Joseph's first dream so many years before, the dream that had infuriated them at the time. Now, "Joseph's brothers came and bowed down before him with their faces to the earth" (Gen. 42:6, NKJV).

Joseph was able to look them in the eyes with true compassion and say to them, "You intended to harm me, but God intended it all for good. He brought me to this position so I could save the lives of many people" (Gen. 50:20, NLT). Sooner or later in your life, you will need a Joseph spirit, a heart that is able to forgive those who hurt you, even when it's your own family. A Joseph spirit can say, "You put me through a lot of bad stuff and you meant it for evil, but what you meant for my evil, God has turned into good. You threw evil at me, but God put a boomerang effect on it and made it turn around, grab up blessings, and come back to me in the form of a blessing. God just used you; that's what it was. And I'm going to bless you from now on."

Joseph's Dream and Your Dream

By the time the brothers came to Egypt, Joseph had lived in Egypt longer than he had been in his father's house in Canaan. He was a mature man of thirty-nine, with high standing in everyone's eyes. He had a wife and children. He was wealthy and strong. But look what he had to go through before he could reach that point.

If you ask yourself, "What does a dream do?" I think one answer that you will come up with is something like this: "A dream will propel you into all sorts of new territory that you never saw before. It will strip you and shake you. You will wonder sometimes if that dream has died. You will almost forget about your dream. But God will always be with you, and His dreams are unforgettable. If you don't give up on your dream, it will come to pass."

All of the things that Joseph had to go through apply to you, especially the parts about evil turning into good. The enemy will laugh at you sometimes. There you are, sitting in some pit or prison that is not of your own making, without any recourse that you can think of. But your God will not allow the enemy to assassinate the dream God has given you.

Did you write down the vision? Did you make it plain in the early stages? Then you can keep running with it. If somebody tries to steal it, you can just put your head down and keep running. You may be panting in desperation, but who wouldn't be? Do not ever give up. If it seems to tarry, do not give up on it. Wait as long as you have to. If your dream seems to die, tell it to live. Watch God resurrect it, maybe more than once. Keep reminding yourself that you can do all things through Christ who strengthens you (Phil. 4:13). Tell yourself that every door that needs to open for you *will* open for you. Remind yourself that you are not going to wander through life, because your dream has become part of your spirit. It used to be a burden, and you didn't know what it could do, but now you know it's a dream, and it's carrying *you*!

REVIEW

Life of Purpose

- God is looking for people to whom He can transfer His passion and dream, people to whom He can give a vision and a dream.

- Every one of His visions and dreams goes through a process of birth, death, and resurrection. God will not allow the enemy to assassinate your dream. Dreams from God are *unforgettable*. They will always come to pass, even if it seems to take forever.

- Let Joseph's story remind you of the stages of the journey of your dream. You will see the harvest field, times of favor and times of disfavor, and the restoration of your dream afterward. You will see how the dreams of others connect with your dream.

- It's not how quickly you get to the fulfillment of your dream; it's how well you finish. Like the torch race in the ancient Greek Olympics, you need to cross the finish line with your flame still burning.

Chapter 3

You Will Come to Vision

I AM NOTORIOUS FOR NOT PAYING ATTENTION to the little red light on the dashboard and running out of gas. You would think I'd learn to fill up.

One Wednesday night during my sermon, I cracked a joke about Dwayne, one of our staff pastors, who had managed somehow miraculously to gain weight during our twenty-one-day fast. That night, I was on my way home when I ran out of gas. I tried calling everybody, purposely avoiding calling Dwayne, even though I knew he would always answer the phone. After many failed attempts at reaching anyone, I had to call Dwayne. He drove out to rescue me, carrying a gas can, with a sly grin on his face.

The very next day, I went to Atlanta with all the family and spent the day there. On the way home, Cherise and I were following our daughters, who were in their car. They sped up and left us behind. Guess what happened? Our car ran out of gas again. There we were on a stretch of road that had no gas stations close by. We called our oldest daughter to come back and get us, which took about twenty-five minutes.

Using her car, I found a gas station. But this particular station didn't have any gas cans or funnels, so I bought a gallon of milk, poured the milk out, and filled it with one gallon of gas. When I got back to the car, Cherise said, "Are you joking? How are you going to get that gas from a milk jug into the tank?" The girls got out their camera phones and began to take pictures of all the creative ways I tried to get the gas into the tank.

First, I tried to just pour it in; it just went all over the side of the car. Next, I grabbed a paper cup from the cup holder in the car, not realizing that the kids had poked holes in the bottom of it. When I put some gas into the cup, it poured out like a fountain all over me. Cherise and the kids were dying laughing. Cherise yelled out, "You are just not cut out for stuff like this!" Then she folded a page out of a magazine to make a funnel, and she was able to get some gas in the car. The whole ordeal took about an hour and a half. All the way home, I pleaded with the kids to not tell anyone about what had happened, but it was too late. They had recorded a video of the incident on their cell phones.

Have you ever felt that your dream was running out of gas? Have you tried everything? How can you funnel some more fuel into your gas tank?

What happens when your vision runs out of gas?

There is a season in everyone's life when your vision "runs out of gas." You *think* you will come to vision. You *hope* you will come to vision, although your vision is certainly not apparent at the moment. You try everything you can to get your dream moving again. Eventually, a shift happens. You figure out how to funnel in some extra gas and get your dream moving again. That's when you become *sure* that you will come to the fulfillment of your vision.

Dreams and visions and destiny are not just for exceptional people like Paul.

That phrase, "I will come to vision" comes from a little line in 2 Corinthians 12: "I will come to visions and revelations of the Lord" (v. 1). It's right before Paul's description of "a man" (it was probably him) who got caught up into the third heaven. With all the description of the third heaven, we don't usually notice that little introductory line, "I will come to visions," but that's what caught my eye one day.

"I will come to vision...*I* will come to vision...I *will* come to vision." Paul did come to his vision.

But wasn't Paul a special case? Can this possibly apply to you and me? Yes, it can—dreams and visions and destiny are not just for exceptional people like Paul. I may not have the same vision as Paul, but I too will come to the particular vision that is the will of God for my life. Like Paul, I will come to "the vision" (singular) and "the visions" (plural) that God has deposited into my spirit. These are the things that God wants me to accomplish. And I will come to a point where I recognize them as being mine, from Him.

Not goal setting

Now, I need to make a distinction here. In a lot of places these days, you hear about goal setting. You hear about it in school and at your job. It seems as if all of the "success stories" talk about goal setting. There's nothing wrong with having goals, but a vision is not the same thing. You set up a goal with your carnal human mind. A vision originates with God. It is a spiritual thing. God puts it in your spirit. And as you tune in to Him, you begin to get clearer about it.

When you begin to come to your vision, you can almost hear God saying, "*This* is the highest you! This is what I see you doing. This is My dream and My vision and My destiny for your life." It will always be bigger than what you thought you could ever do or be. It will always be impossible to achieve without the continual help of the Holy Spirit.

But it's not your idea in the first place. It is His. It is God's idea for you.

I understand how it feels to be unsure of your vision. You are always wondering, "Is it going to happen?" and you're hoping and wishing that something could happen. But a time will come when you move out of the hoping and wishing and thinking realm into the "it *is* going to happen" realm.

When you begin to come to your vision, you can almost hear God saying, "This is the highest you!"

That's what happened for Paul. Something shifted. After that, he could say affirmatively, "I will come to vision!" His faith suddenly took a quantum leap, and he actually believed God was going to take him someplace he'd never been before. The same thing will happen for you. It's as if your spirit glimpses the reality God has for you, and then it catches its breath. Suddenly you realize that you're about to step out into something that is beyond yourself. You find that you too are coming to the vision God planted in your spirit. It doesn't matter anymore what the devil may have tried to put in the way. You *will* come to vision.

What is the thing you're hoping against hope for? That thing you can hardly pray about because it seems to be so out of reach? But you *have* prayed. You have prayed in secret. And you have thought about it a lot. You have wished for it even if you haven't been brave enough to tell anybody about it.

With Paul, he couldn't even tell people about it directly after he reached it, he was so humbled by this experience. He was caught up into a higher place. It changed him. After that, he walked straighter. He was much more sure of how God saw him. He could share the inspiration with others. He could write in his letter to the Corinthians: "I will come to visions."

He had turned a corner. Now he knew for sure. A lot of the outer details of his life stayed the same. He was still buffeted by circumstances. (You will be too.) He still didn't see the complete

47

fulfillment of his dream. But his faith had been ignited as never before. He had come to vision.

I feel led by the Holy Spirit to tell you that no matter what you're dealing with right now, you will come to vision. Hell can't stop it; demons can't stop it—you will come to vision!

Now, you may not have a vision to be in the fivefold ministry— preaching, teaching, and all of that. (You may, though.) We all have different calls; not all of us are supposed be preachers or on staff at a church or ministry. Some of you are called to be surgeons or nurses or businesspeople or mechanics. But if you belong to God and you will not quit, you will come to vision.

The way you know that you're called is that you can't do anything else and be happy. Then you know you're really called! If you had a million dollars, a mansion, and a beautiful car, would that make you happy? Would those things make you feel fulfilled? I'm sure it would be wonderful, but let me tell you, it would not be enough for this preacher because, "Woe is unto me, if I preach not the gospel" (1 Cor. 9:16). That's how the call of God is. I cannot be happy in any other place.

When He calls you to the missionary field, or when He calls you to be an evangelist, or to build a corporation, then you cannot get away from it. "For the gifts and calling of God are without repentance" (Rom. 11:29). Your God-given destiny is "without repentance." That means you cannot get away from it.

Just say, "God, give me Your intentions. Give me Your intentions." Give Him permission to bring you to your vision. Some of you are going to have a dream to be a secretary. Some of you are going to want to do things that are hidden and that seem insignificant. But I have news for you—if it is God's plan for your life, it is awesome!

Application

You have to *apply* to know your vision, the same way you might apply for a job. You can't just float through life and expect your vision to happen to you.

You must believe that all things are possible—even in your own life. You must raise your eyes up off the floor and fix them on Him. Ask Him to give you your vision. Apply for it. Tell Him, "God, I want Your dream." Seek His will today and every day. And when it seems to have been taken away from you, speak life back into your dream. Say to it, "Live, dream, *live*. Live, live, live!"

Don't be passive. Don't be a floater kind of person. If you are just floating through life, life will chew you up and spit you out.

Instead, be active. Lay hold of your dream, because having a dream will make you disciplined. It will give you the power you need to look at temptations and say, "No—that would mess up my dream. No—I know where I'm going, and it's not that direction. That way will get me off track."

As long as Samson had a dream, he was unconquerable. When he lost his vision, he was conquered by a ninety-pound Delilah. When David had a dream, he was undefeatable, but when he lost his dream, he fell to the sexual temptation of adultery. You need a dream to keep you focused and disciplined.

Four Consequences of a Dream

Standing before King Agrippa, the apostle Paul said, "I was not disobedient unto the heavenly vision" (Acts 26:19). In other words, "God gave me a vision, and I was not disobedient to it." Paul was saying, "In spite of the setbacks [because they will come to any dream], in spite of the hardships, in spite of the trouble and the adversity, I was not disobedient to the heavenly vision."

Paul was not disobedient to his vision from God because along with the vision, God did four things for Paul. When you get a vision from God for your life, He absolutely will do these same four things for you!

The vision *stops* you.

On the road to Damascus, the vision stopped Paul. You know the story. In the middle of the day, he's riding his horse, and he had a Sonstroke. Not s-u-n stroke, but a S-o-n stroke. The Son of God appeared to him as bright as the noonday sun and knocked Paul off his horse. Suddenly, he was stopped.

Something will happen to you when you find God's perfect will, purpose, and plan for your life. It will stop you in your tracks. You may be totally happy doing what you're doing, and then, all of a sudden, it just hits you, and instantly everything is changed. The vision stops you.

The vision *sends* you.

"*Go*, for he is a chosen vessel of Mine to bear My name before Gentiles, kings, and the children of Israel. For I will show him how many things he must suffer for My name's sake" (Acts 9:15–16, NKJV, emphasis mine). This was God's prophetic word over Paul in Damascus.

Not only did Paul's vision *stop* him from what he was doing, but it also *sent* him to Rome and to other nations to stand before great kings and be a witness for Christ. When you get a real vision from God about your life, it will send you someplace. It will send you to other people. That's one way you can tell the difference between vision and ambition. Vision comes from God, and it will make you help people; ambition comes from your flesh, and it will make you use people. You can't confuse vision with ambition, because there's such a big difference.

I'm not saying that there's anything wrong with having the ambition you need to achieve success. There's nothing wrong with wanting to be, say, a successful businessperson, if you tie your success to helping other people and building the kingdom of God. There's nothing wrong with wanting to be a person of great influence, or dreaming of being a famous athlete, or an incredible governor, or a good lawyer, or president of the United States, as long as it is tied back to helping other people and glorifying God and building the kingdom.

When God promotes you, His vision is not so you can say, "Look at me," but it is so that you can use your influence to touch other people. A God-given vision will send you to new places and new faces.

The vision *strengthens* you.

First, God sent a vision that stopped Paul, and then He sent him. Then, just as important as those two, God gave Paul the strength he needed to carry the vision out—for years and years, through all sorts of setbacks. He will do the same for you so that when adversity comes, when all hell is breaking loose, you will have the strength to get up and keep on going. Only a real vision and a real dream can do that!

I have never talked to anybody who's done anything of any significance and has not hit days, weeks, and months when they had to plow through all kinds of opposition. It just comes with the territory.

A God-breathed vision puts strength right into you. Then you can go on and press on in spite of everything! The Bible says that Jesus, "for the joy that was set before him endured the cross, despising the shame" (Heb. 12:2). He had supernatural determination. Even while those soldiers were nailing Him, He endured it. They were nailing Him, and He didn't let the temporary attack of nails and flogging keep Him from fulfilling the greatest vision ever given by the Father to anyone.

He was looking out there to the joy while they were killing Him. He was looking to the joy while they were pounding His hands and feet onto the cross. For the joy that was set before Him, He endured the searing pain, the abandonment, the certainty of death! He could see the vision. "I can endure the cross today because I know where I'm going tomorrow!" It strengthened Him so that He could make it to His tomorrow. Have you ever thought of that before? It applies to our smaller circumstances too. "Where I am right now is not where I am going."

When Paul said that he was not disobedient to the heavenly vision, what kinds of challenges to his obedience had he faced? Look at this list of potential setbacks and difficult circumstances. God must have sent him more-than-adequate strength to go through more-than-average trials: endless travel over all kinds of terrain on foot and by other difficult and unsafe means, backbreaking labor, imprisonment, beatings and whippings and stonings, death threats, three shipwrecks, sleeplessness and cold, hunger and thirst, and poverty. (See the whole long list in 2 Corinthians 11:23–28.)

Yes, he went through all of that and more, but Paul the great apostle thinks of it as the "small print" of his life. He calls it a "light affliction": "Though our outward man is perishing, yet the inward man is renewed day by day. For our light affliction, which is but for a moment, is working for us a far more exceeding and eternal weight of glory" (2 Cor. 4:16–17, NKJV).

In that same chapter, before Paul said to Agrippa, "I was not disobedient unto the heavenly vision" (Acts 26:19), he looked at the evil king and said, "I think myself happy…" (v. 2). I love that verse! I want to write a book called *I Think Myself Happy.* Isn't that a good title? You know how it works: if you think you're going to get depressed, you think yourself depressed. "I'm depressed." Why? Because you're thinking about it. Well, it's time to think yourself happy! Doesn't it just make you start to get happy just to *think* happy right now?

So, Paul went through all this stuff, and what helped him through it? A great vision. His dream was much bigger than the small print of life. He could think happy because of God's call on his life.

The vision *stretches* you.

Paul's dream stretched him. The dream enlarged him. The vision helped him become what he would never have become without it. It showed him that the journey is more important than the destination.

Real, anointed praise is when you remember what you came through.

It's like the Olympics. When those athletes stand and get their gold medals, they'll often break down crying. They're not crying over that moment of getting the medal around their necks;

they're thinking about all the stuff they had to go through to get there: the blisters on their hands, the torn ligaments, the many times they couldn't go out like the other kids because they were in training. They're not thinking about the moment of the prize; they're thinking about the journey.

That's what praise is. You don't just praise Him because you feel good right now. (You might not feel so good right now.) But real, anointed praise is when you remember what you came through. You made it! "Yeah, I'm a little emotional because I didn't know if I was going to make it, but I made it. Praise be to God!"

Have you ever given God some gold-medal praise? Maybe other people didn't understand. "Why?" they wonder. "The song wasn't *that* good." They don't understand that you're not into just that moment; you're thinking of what you went through. Something once broke your heart, and you thought you weren't going to make it through, but God was faithful, and now you're just feeling overwhelmed with the gold medal. It stretches you.

The vision God gives you will stretch you. Studies show that the average person only uses 5 percent of his or her mental ability. Many people do not ever put themselves in situations that force them to stretch their faith, talent, or resources. A rubber band is not effective unless it's stretched. In fact, you could say that a rubber band never fulfills its purpose until it's stretched.

The same is true with us. What's stretching you right now? Are you in a job that's stretching you? Or are you just in a place of contentment and at ease? "Woe to them that are at ease in Zion" (Amos 6:1).

Paul's dream stretched him; the dream enlarged him. The God-given vision helped him become what he would never have become without it. Most people try to avoid stretching. That's why God often has to bring motivation of some kind before we will stretch. We won't do it naturally.

I once heard a story about a multimillionaire in Texas who was having an outdoor barbecue in the backyard of his massive ranch. Hundreds of guests were there at this prestigious event. He asked some of the men to walk down to the swimming pool with him. When they arrived, they were shocked to see his pool full of alligators. Someone asked him why. He explained that the number-one quality he admired most in a person was courage. So he had made a vow to give one-half of his vast fortune to any man who would swim the length of the alligator-infested pool. As they turned around and started walking back toward the ranch, suddenly there was a splash. When they turned back around, they were astonished to see one of their group swimming as fast as he could with the alligators chasing and snapping at him. Somehow, the swimmer managed to get to the other side of the pool in one piece. The millionaire was so impressed, he slapped the man on the back and said, "I've never seen such courage and bravery in all my life. I will give you up to half of all that I own. Just tell me what you want." The man replied, "I just want to find the person who pushed me into the water!"

Have you ever had God push you into something you would have never voluntarily jumped into? Success is facing the challenges of life and not shrinking back from them. Every person God has ever used had to stretch. When Elisha prayed for the dead boy, he "stretched himself upon the child" (2 Kings 4:34). After the stretch came a miracle! In order to get a miracle, it will require you to stretch your faith and actions like never before.

Success is facing the challenges of life
and not shrinking back from them.

John F. Kennedy told this story about his great-grandfather, Thomas Fitzgerald, who grew up in Ireland. In the country, they had rough, jagged stone walls that separated people's fields. When he was a little boy, he and his friends liked to climb those walls. Sometimes it was almost too difficult. So, to make himself do it, Fitzgerald would toss his little cap over the wall so he wouldn't have a choice. It motivated him. "Now I've got to do it. I can't go home without my cap." I think some of us need to do the same thing. If we throw our "cap" over the wall or mountain or obstacle that we're facing, we motivate ourselves to try harder, to stretch. Our action also puts the enemy on notice that we do not intend to quit. Whatever we do, we intend to succeed, because something important to us is already over there.

Most people are vulnerable when they are stretching. Just as a rubber band is more likely to snap when it's stretched, the same is true when you stretch to reach your God-given vision. You're vulnerable when your dream is making you stretch.

Remember that every person who has ever stretched has been tempted to cease stretching because they're discouraged. They need to get around others who will encourage them. The easiest way to get some encouragement is to give it. David had Jonathan. Jonathan encouraged David. (See 1 Samuel 23:16.) But even when he didn't have Jonathan anymore, the Bible says that David "encouraged himself in the Lord" (1 Sam. 30:6). He didn't want to quit, even though he was discouraged. He knew this truth: when we stop stretching, the people around us stop stretching.

Most people need affirmation when they're stretching. The most important time to encourage people is when they're taking a risk. If you're ever going to be a cheerleader or a backslapper, this is the time to do it. Most people affirm too late.

Another thing most people never learn is that the stretching is never supposed to stop. One word you'll never find in the Bible is *retirement*. You're supposed to stretch and stretch and stretch for the rest of your life.

Believe in Yourself

Before you can discover what God has called you to do or you reach your full potential, you have to find a lasting basis on which to build your self-worth. Just as your beliefs can move you forward, your shadow beliefs can hold you back. What are shadow beliefs? That's the committee in your head that tells you that you're not able, not worthy, or that you'll never make it.

What are your shadow beliefs? Today, I challenge you to bring them out into the light and expose them to God's Word. Don't let them control you or decide your future. Refuse to translate any thought into a word if it contradicts what God says about you. You can't speak death over your dreams and expect to see them come to life.

Paul says, "He chose us in Him before the foundation of the world" (Eph. 1:4, NKJV). Even if nobody valued you or showed you love in any way, this verse shatters and dispels all rejection by letting you know that God chose you. Imagine, you're called by God and hand-crafted for a specific purpose at precisely this time and in precisely this location! Wow! You came precut to fill a particular place that nobody else could fill. You were selected.

So, stop trying to be like somebody else! If you give up being who you are in order to become like them, you'll end up being somebody God doesn't need one more of. He made you in a precise way, for a precise purpose, and only you will do. Think about this: regardless of what you like or dislike about yourself, you must be OK because God chose you. Stop doubting yourself or competing with others. Nobody can take what God has reserved for you! Today you have a choice; either let others determine your worth, or let God.

In Genesis 1:31 we read, "Then God saw everything that He had made, and indeed it was very good" (NKJV). Before you were born, God saw you. He knew the specific purpose you were designed to fulfill, so He provided you with the gifts you would need. Then, He looked at you and said, "Very good."

Today you have a choice; either let others determine your worth, or let God.

Can you say that too about yourself? It's important that you can, because others will only treat you according to how you treat yourself. If you don't like the way people respond to you, stop and ask yourself, "What's the message I'm sending?" In order to be treated well, you have to send a message that says, "I'm somebody because God made me somebody. Therefore, I feel good about me."

We're talking here about inner strength that makes you attractive when you walk into a room and causes others to say, "Who's that?" They're not asking because of your physical appearance but because your presence has impact. This is not pride; it's just healthy self-esteem based on God's opinion of you. It's what I call God-esteem! When you have it, it affects the way you talk to others, apply for a job, perform a ministry, or even how you pray. That's right; if you think you have no value, you'll pray with less faith and conclude that the promises of God are for everybody but you.

Appreciate who God made you to be, and develop what He gave you. Stop wishing you were somebody else. You have a unique blend of gifts and talents. You have a special destiny on Earth.

Gideon is an example of somebody who wasn't exactly standing in a volunteer line. He wasn't looking to be stretched or to be used by God. In fact, he was hiding in a dry winepress for fear of his Midianite enemies. Then, along came God's angel, saying, "You are a mighty man of valor!" (See Judges 6:12.) Gideon did not feel like a mighty man of valor, but God had sent the angel to help him see himself that way.

The story goes on to tell how he assembled his army. When he blew a trumpet, 32,000 Israelites showed up to fight the Midianite army. Actually, that wasn't so impressive. The Midianites had 250,000 men, so 32,000 was just a drop in the bucket.

What did God decide to do? It was unbelievable. He decided to make the army smaller. First, He had Gideon "disinvite" the ones who were afraid, which was a lot of them—22,000 to be exact. Now the army was down to 10,000 (and the Midianite army had not decreased at all).

You see, sometimes God will diminish you to deliver you. It may seem like you're being diminished in some way in your life. Anytime God reduces you numerically, it's to drive you back to your source. There's no greater or safer place to be than right in the center of God's will, even if that place seems to be a place of disadvantage. With God there is such a thing as blessed subtractions. That's when He diminishes you to develop your faith in Him.

You remember the story (Judg. 7). Gideon obeyed when God told him to bring the men down to the water to drink. And he watched how they drank. The ones who used their hands to scoop up the water were the ones God would use to bring about the victory. Now, out of 10,000, only 300 were left.

Why scooping? I think it's because the men who used their hands to scoop up the water had to have empty hands. They had to lay aside their weapons in order to scoop the water in their cupped palms. It's as if God were saying, "Come to Me with empty hands. Put down your carnal weapons. I'm not going to use whatever you have been depending on to win this battle."

Besides that, the ones who scooped the water ended up with clean hands. God wants to use people who have empty, clean hands! Clean hands represent a level of consecration and holiness that is required when God wants to use you against the devil. He wants to use people who will obey without hesitation.

Finally, Gideon came to the realization that it was "not by might, nor by power, but by my spirit, saith the LORD of hosts" (Zech. 4:6). He realized that God had reduced his numbers so that he would understand that numbers were never where his strength lay in the first place. God was his refuge. God was his strength.

You need to be careful about putting your confidence in numbers. Remember, David suffered his most significant judgment when he numbered Israel (2 Sam. 24). There are two things to remember about numbers. When it comes to God:

- Never allow numbers to worship you.
- Never allow yourself to worship numbers.

God alone held the victory in His mighty hand. Gideon's weakness would not be exploited by the enemy. Instead, it would be used by the Lord of hosts to display His magnificent power.

The devil's worst nightmare

Then what did God tell Gideon to do? He said, "I want you to go and to hear what's going on in the enemy camp." So Gideon got his servant to go with him, and they sneaked down to the enemy camp. (See Judges 7:13–15.)

This was a strange instruction. In order to make it possible for Gideon to have enough confidence, God was sending him to hear what his enemies were saying about him. He wanted him to see himself through God's eyes—and through the enemy's eyes. It's the same for you. If you can see yourself through the enemy's eyes, your confidence will increase.

God needed Gideon to believe that he could do what He had told him. So, in order to build his confidence, God said, "Hide behind the bush and eavesdrop on what the Midianites are saying about your potential."

The devil's worst nightmare is that you and I are going to wake up and recognize our authority in Christ.

That's how he heard about the nightmare. One of the enemy soldiers had just had a nightmare about his invasion. The barley cake in the nightmare represented Gideon's army, and it also represents the bread or Word of God. One word from the Lord causes the devil to have nightmares. One person, somebody like Gideon, who doesn't have anything to start with—no money, no power, no nothing—can demolish the enemy's stronghold with a single word from God.

Get your mind around this. The devil's worst nightmare is that you and I are going to wake up and recognize our authority in Christ instead of going around muttering, "I am the least of the brethren. I am the least of the tribes. I have so much against me." When you and I discover what our purpose is and how God wants us to approach the battle for victory, we'll know already that we have won, and *that* will make the devil worried.

That's the way it should be, don't you think? It should be the case that the forces in the enemy camp are the ones who are worried—not the Lord's anointed. It's too often the other way around; the wrong camp is worrying.

The devil's worst nightmare is that you will look beyond the earthly view and see through the eyes of heaven, as Gideon did when he heard what was taking place in the enemy's camp. The enemy knows he is defeated, and he's desperately hoping that you don't know it. The devil's worst nightmare is that you and I will get an understanding of what they're saying in the enemy's camp right now about us. When Gideon heard how fearful his enemy was of him, it boosted his faith to a place where he could say, "I believe that I can do anything." And guess what. As a man thinks, so is he (Prov. 23:7). What have your enemy and his imps been saying about you and your potential? I assure you it would shock you to know.

I remember that when the Lord called me to preach, I felt like Gideon. I felt like he did when he said, "I am poor. I am of the small tribe of Benjamin. I'm the youngest in my family." (See

Judges 6:15.) In other words, "I'm just the runt of the litter; I'm a nobody." That's a self-defeating attitude if I ever saw one, but it's not uncommon. That's what some of you are saying in your battle: "I'm defeated; I don't have anything. I'm not supertalented. I'm not special; I'm just average."

Meanwhile, over in the enemy's camp they're having nightmares about you. Their only hope is if you stay stuck in your old way of thinking. If you don't respond to God's dream for your life, then the enemy wins. If he can make you think you misheard God, maybe he can still prevail.

I want to tell you that you are more important than you think you are. Important people do important things. Believe that you can. Build that business, get that degree, launch that ministry, birth that dream. If you can believe it, you can be it.

Don't quit.

This is no time to back up. This is no time to be discouraged. This is no time to "process" what's happening to you. This is a time to say, "God, show me who I really am in You and what I'm capable of."

This is the time to see things a different way. Gideon led his puny army into battle with 300 men against 250,000, and all they had were a trumpet and breakable pitchers that held a candle of fire. When Gideon said, "Break the jars," those torches flared up. (See Judges 7:19.) The enemy camp flew into a panic, and they started killing everything in sight—which was each other! Gideon and his little army must have just stood there in the torchlight with their mouths hanging open. (See Judges 7:22–23.)

You see, the breaking of the glass pitchers represents a willingness to be broken so that God's light can shine forth. His dream for your life can be fulfilled, even in the face of insurmountable odds. Can God break you and you'll still trust Him enough to pick up the trumpet of praise and glorify Him? Can you go through a breaking experience—a financial setback, a divorce, a job loss—and still maintain your torch of holy fire?

Then you will come to vision. You will believe that you can achieve it. You will take hold of the power of your dream, the destiny that God poured into your spirit when He created you.

REVIEW

You Will Come to Vision

- God is the giver of visions. Ask Him for yours.

- Visions do four things: they stop you, send you, strengthen you, and stretch you.

- Let Gideon's story remind you about three things: how God sees you, the importance of obedience, and the power of brokenness.

- Remember—the enemy should be the one having nightmares, not you!

Chapter 4

TAKE HOLD OF
YOUR DREAM

WELL, IF SOMEBODY WOULD GIVE

me a break in life, I could

achieve something." How often have you heard (or

said) something like that? How often do people

just stick their hands in their pockets and watch

65

life go by, waiting for their lucky moment, feeling like they're relegated to the sidelines.

Finding out God's will for your life shouldn't depend on "luck" or "fate." And regardless of how your life has treated you, His will for you *isn't* to give up on you and throw you in the trash. He's not limited by your life circumstances. After all, this is the same God who took nothing and made it into something—this whole big world! He can, and will, do the same thing with your life, even if you think your life is just a big zero.

You have hope, Mr. or Ms. Zero, if you are connected to Jehovah God, because He specializes in taking nothing and nobody and making something beautiful out of it.

Here's why:

> The race is not to the swift,
> Nor the battle to the strong,
> Nor bread to the wise,
> Nor riches to men of understanding,
> Nor favor to men of skill;
> But *time and chance happen to them all.*
> For man also does not know his time:
> *Like fish taken in a cruel net,*
> *Like birds caught in a snare,*
> *So the sons of men are snared in an evil time,*
> When it falls suddenly upon them.
>
> —ECCLESIASTES 9:11–12, NKJV, EMPHASIS MINE

"Time and chance happen to them all." Another way of saying it is this: God gives *everybody* a shot at destiny. He created you for something. He didn't create you just to take up space on Earth for a while and use up a little oxygen. Do you want to be a difference maker or a space taker?

Colliding with your destiny

Time and chance happen to us all. Do you know what the word *chance* means in this context? It means "to collide with your destiny." This means that you are headed for a collision with God's will for your life. He has prearranged for you to have a collision with your destiny.

Right before you were created, there was one little sperm among millions of them, all racing to become *you*. Millions of them were swimming, trying to get to that egg. And you won. This makes you one in a million! You're a winner, not an accident. I don't care if you came from an illegitimate birth. No seed and egg can come together and come to full-term life unless God gives life. Nobody is a loser. Every single life has a destiny. God wants each of us to collide with our destiny. He wants us to know why we were born.

So, there's a promise and a warning in these words. The promise is that every one of us has a God-ordained destiny. The warning is that you can miss your destiny when the right moment comes if you are entangled in something you have no business being involved in.

Your destiny is connected to a specific, and "evil," time. "For man also does not know his time: like fish taken in a cruel net, like birds caught in a snare, so the sons of men are snared in an evil time" (Eccles. 9:12, NKJV). God's warning to you is not to be distracted or mixed up in Satan's traps when you are colliding with destiny or you could miss your moment forever. Satan becomes active in your life when he sees that you are about to take hold of your destiny. Satan tries to throw over you every net he can lay his hands on.

A net is anything that confines and controls you, anything that holds you back from moving on with God. It may be a net of addiction, alcohol or drugs, or a net of offense and unforgiveness. You don't want to be tangled up in a net or else you may miss your chance for freedom. If they're entangled in a net, fish can't swim, birds can't fly—and you can't fulfill your dream or destiny.

Satan becomes active in your life when he sees that you are about to take hold of your destiny.

I see young people doing their own thing. They tell themselves, "I'll come to Christ when I get ready. I'll have some fun first." They're tangled up in a net of popularity or partying or peer pressure. Others get into nets of wrong relationships and miss their moment of destiny.

"The chance and the time" is already preordained. It's ready for each and every person. But if you're tied up in a net of sin and bondage and bitterness, it will keep you back. Ask God to do something about it. Ask Him to do as He did for Andrew, who was involved with his fishing nets when Jesus walked up to him and said two words: "Follow Me." (See Matthew 4:18–20.) Andrew had never seen Him before. Jesus didn't wait for an answer. He didn't give him much time to think. He just said, "Follow Me."

And Andrew dropped his nets and followed Him. What would have happened if he had been tangled up in his nets?

Andrew did not miss his collision with destiny. When his destiny came knocking, he didn't keep his hands in his nets. He grabbed hold of his future and became one of Jesus's disciples. The whole kingdom of God was wrapped up in that moment.

I've known people who couldn't fulfill the call of God to go into all the world and preach the gospel because they were so entangled in the net of financial debt. We've all known single people who were so entangled in a wrong relationship that they couldn't look up when Mr. or Miss Right came along.

Don't let any kind of net hold you back. What nets are you tangled up in that could potentially stop you from doing what God has designed for you to do? Drop the net and follow Jesus. This is your season for a collision with destiny.

Six Stages to Every Dream

I want to give you the sequence of how your dream or vision will unfold so that you can grab hold of each step as it occurs. I have identified six stages in the sequence:

1. I thought it.
2. I caught it.
3. I bought it.
4. I sought it.
5. I got it.
6. I taught it.

These are the six stages of how a dream gets birthed inside of you. Let's look at each of them in turn.

I thought it.

This first stage is like what I said in the previous chapter—it may be just a thought, something that doesn't mean much to the people around you, but to you it's like a revelation. It just won't let you go.

You turn that thought over and over in your mind. "Man, could I really do that? I *could* do that! I can see myself doing that. It could really happen."

I caught it.

You can't stay at the first stage forever. In fact, if you turn that thought over in your mind enough, it's almost inevitable that you will catch hold of it and begin to talk to other people about it. You don't present it as if it's a done deal; you just kind of throw the idea out there and explore the possibility of it. Now it begins to be more than a thought.

Now that you're talking about it, you've "caught" it. You're talking about it. You're actually looking into it. You've gone beyond thinking about it.

These two stages may sound familiar to you. Most people get this far. But too often, somewhere between stage two and stage three, their dream dies. They don't go on to the next step.

I bought it.

Step three is the "I bought it" stage. That's where you have to pay the price. That's the stage beyond talk (which is free). Now you have to put it on the line. You have to buy into the dream and take a little risk. You decide that your old life is just too boring, and you decide to take a risk. You decide that you've circled this same mountain long enough, and you go in to conquer it. You step out on your idea to see if it's strong enough to hold up.

You believe that with God, all things are possible. You begin to pay the price in terms of education and in terms of equipping yourself for fulfilling your dream. Somebody has said, "The tassel is worth the hassle." You do whatever you have to do. You say, "I'm getting out of this boat. I'm going for it. I'm sweating and I'm tired and I'm working two jobs, but I'm doing this. I'm buying in!" You know that if there's no weeping, there's no reaping.

I sought it.

After you buy into your dream and put some sweat equity into it, then you really get committed. Now nobody can talk you out of it. You're like a maniac on a mission. You can't think of anything else. Your kinfolk can't even stop you. You have that look in your eye; you have the eye of the tiger on the hunt.

I got it.

Now you're there! You grab hold of the whole prize! You've paid the price, and you've walked the walk. And you're glad you did.

Now you won't have to suffer the cancer of life—which is called "regret." My worst nightmare is to be sitting in a rocking chair forty years from now, saying, "What if...?" When I'm an old man, I don't want to look back on my life and see a bunch of lost dreams. I want to be able to say, "I got it!" I got this one, and I got that one too.

I taught it.

There is no success without a successor. Paul had Timothy. Elijah had Elisha. Moses had Joshua. Whom are you mentoring, and who is mentoring you?

I have an amazing mother, Kay Franklin Lancaster. She is one of twenty-seven children! That's right; she has twenty-six brothers and sisters. She has taught me so much about the things of God. Any success I've had in the ministry I would say is in large part because of her godly influence.

> *Whom are you mentoring, and*
> *who is mentoring you?*

My dad used to pastor a little church of thirty to forty members in North Carolina. In order to make ends meet and stay in the ministry, he had to subsidize his pay by selling food to factory workers. When money was running low, Mom would get up and fix homemade biscuits and sausage. Dad had an old pickup truck with a camper on the back. He painted on the side of the camper, "Bill's Meals on Wheels." At 4:30 in the morning he would drive up to the cotton mills and furniture mills and sell biscuits like hotcakes out of the back of the camper on the truck. I'm blessed today because of the amazing sacrifices my parents made to keep our family in full-time ministry. They not only believed, but they also taught me to believe that I can!

REVIEW

Take Hold of Your Dream

⊚ God created you for something. You have a destiny, and He wants you to know what it is and to take hold of it.

⊚ Most often, you will discover your destiny in six stages: "I thought it, I caught it, I bought it, I sought it, I got it, and I taught it."

⊚ Once you've grabbed hold of your dream, hang on to it in spite of the doubts and difficulties that beset you. Disentangle yourself from whatever holds you back.

⊚ Trust God all the way. Keep your focus on Him. He will make a way for your dream to come true.

Chapter 5

UNFOLDING YOUR DREAM

I've always had a desire to do something for God.

I have been in church all my life, from the time I was too little to know anything. I remember sitting on my mother's lap and sometimes lying in the pew during services. Somewhere in the midst of those early years, something got hold of me that I now call "desire."

One way it showed was with music. When I was eight or nine years old, I got some empty shoeboxes, and I made myself some drumsticks out of pieces of old coat hangers. I would listen to the gospel music records that Mom and Dad had, and I would beat my "drums" to the tune of whatever music was playing.

One day my daddy walked in and said, "Since you want to play the drums that bad, I'm going to buy you a drum set, boy." He did, and he moved them into his church. We didn't have a drummer in our church, and I didn't really know how to play. I was scared to death. But I had a *desire* to play the drums for God, and I did.

Then, a few years later, I went to my mom and said, "Mom, I heard a saxophone on a record, and I want to play one." She bought me a saxophone. I don't know why, but I became obsessed with playing the saxophone. It would prove to be a major part of my life.

I received a full scholarship to college based on my ability to play the sax. Later in life, when I began to evangelize, one of the things that helped me was the fact that I not only preached but also played a pretty mean sax. Doors began to open for me. One day, the largest Christian television network in the world invited me to come play my sax on their program. This opportunity began to give me national and international exposure. It gave me the opportunity to preach on that network every week, reaching millions of people. But it all started with an unexplainable desire to play the sax.

Then, I would go on fasts for two days and three days and twenty-one days. Why would anybody do something like that? The Lord spoke to me and said, "It is your *desire* that impresses Me. It wasn't that you pushed the food back, but it was the fact that you *desired* something from Me."

There's no substitute for desire.

It begins with desire.

The point I'm trying to make is that it doesn't begin with talent; it begins with desire. Then, one thing can lead to another. You have to have the desire first or you won't do anything. You have to want it. There's no substitute for desire. You know the verse: "One thing have I desired of the LORD, that will I seek after..." (Ps. 27:4).

Louis Braille lost both eyes at the age of three in an accident in his father's harness shop. But he had a desire. He said, "I'll make a system so that the blind can read and write." He wanted to read and write, so he invented the system that's named after him, the Braille system. He had the desire to do it.

The apostle Paul, traveling on foot mostly, covered Asia in the space of two and a half years. He didn't have an airplane, a car, or a train. He didn't have a TV show. It wasn't easy. All he had was his desire to do it in obedience to the Spirit of God. People tried to stop him, but Paul's desire was to preach in as many places as he could reach, and he didn't care if that was a prison or a palace. He wanted to finish the race with a clear conscience, having fulfilled his desire and the desire of His Lord Jesus. "I press on, that I may lay hold of that for which Christ Jesus has also laid hold of me....I press toward the goal for the prize of the upward call of God in Christ Jesus" (Phil. 3:12, 14, NKJV). His *desire* propelled him onward.

There's always something to hold you back if you let it. There's always an excuse you can give as to why you can't do what God has called you to do. There's always some embarrassing situation or something you have to get over. But if you have *desire*, you can say, with Paul, "None of these things move me."

> *When God calls you to do something,*
> *He prepares you in advance.*

What are the things that didn't move Paul? It was all those things he listed in 2 Corinthians 11: beatings and stonings and all kinds of hardship and dangers. The apostle Paul was not deterred by the fact that he was not tall and handsome, or that he was not suave or photogenic, or that he was not Mr. Personality. The Bible says that his presence was weak. Apparently, the way he came across to people was weak and contemptible (2 Cor. 10:10).

But he pressed on past all these things, because he had the desire. He didn't make excuses.

No excuses

You were born with an assignment. Don't die until you've fulfilled it. Your God-given assignment will always tug at your heart and lead you to your highest fulfillment. Your assignment will unlock your compassion and creativity.

When God calls you to do something, He prepares you in advance. By the time I preached my first sermon I was steeped in church, and all my heroes were preachers. At the time I saw no way to get from the lowly pew where I sat to the pulpit I admired so much, yet God had created within me a desire for ministry, and desire is always the first step toward destiny.

Do you remember how the different tribes of Israel responded to Deborah and Barak when they called them to battle? They wrote a song about it, and that's how we know about the excuses that three of the tribes made. In the song, after they praised the tribes that did come and help in the battle, they wrote a second verse about the tribes that *didn't* show up and fight—Reuben, Dan, and Asher. Why didn't they come? What were their excuses?

"In the tribe of Reuben there was great indecision..." (Judg. 5:15, NLT). In other words, when the messenger came to the tribe of Reuben to ask for their help, the leaders must have called a committee meeting. They must have said, "Let's have a study. Let's get some reports. Let's figure out and rationalize whether or not we should join this battle." After all that, they didn't respond to the invitation.

Then there was the tribe of Dan. The song says, "Why did Dan remain in ships?" (Judg. 5:17). These guys were merchants who carried their merchandise in ships on the sea. It's like they had floating department stores. They were businessmen. When the messenger came to ask them to help fight in the battle, the head of the tribe of Dan, whose priority was his business, said, "Tell Deborah we're sorry. Tell her we'll be there in spirit, but our business is doing real well right now, and our priorities are right here." They didn't respond to the invitation either.

There was one other tribe, the tribe of Asher. The song goes on, "Asher continued on the sea shore" (Judg. 5:17). Was Asher on vacation or what? Here it was, time to assemble and fight, time to run with Deborah's vision, and all of Asher's folks are taking their leisure at the beach. Now, there's nothing wrong with being on vacation, but this definitely was not the time for one. I'm sure they were like some people who say, "I just need a break." If they're not careful, the enemy will make their break turn into a permanent vacation from the purposes of God.

Don't let your weakness or your feelings undermine your desire. Instead, fan the flames of your desire. It's one of the most important parts of responding to God's vision for your life.

Desire plus *passion* equals power.

Have you ever wondered if there was one quality, one distinguishing characteristic, one accomplishment in your life that can excite God more than any other? One thing that can make one person succeed where another fails? One thing that can take you from mediocrity to excellence? One thing that can infuse your life with power and purpose? One thing that sets "great" leaders apart from "average" leaders?

Well, there is, and it is not background, giftedness, or good looks. It is *passion*. God loves a person of passion. He will pass up the crowd for the person whose heart is burning with passion, zeal, desire, and holy fire.

Jesus said, "The zeal of my Father's house has eaten me up." (See Psalm 69:9.) What is eating you up? What fires you up? Where is your desire? Where is your passion?

God will pass up the crowd for the person whose heart is burning with passion, zeal, desire, and holy fire.

The word *desire* means consuming passion. Unrelenting. Undying drive. Insatiable hunger. Unquenchable thirst. Intense fervency. We've all known people who were quiet, laid back, and mediocre until you touch that one thing they're passionate about, and suddenly they come alive. They rise out of obscurity, no longer wallflowers, but more like heat-seeking missiles.

Passion will take you places and cause you to do things you would never do without it. I want to talk to you about some characteristics of a few people in the Bible who saw miraculous power demonstrated in their lives. In each one, you will find an overwhelming *passion*. The key to unleashing God's power is a preceding, overriding passion for Him. There must be passion to ignite the release of His explosive power.

When God sees passion in people, He releases His power through them. I encourage you to follow the example of passionate people such as Elijah, the twelve disciples, and Jesus Himself. Then, apply these principles to your life. When you do, you will see a life-transforming spirit of power and victory take up residence in your soul. Remember, *power follows passion.*

Jesus, a portrait of passion

It was "after his passion" (Acts 1:3) that Jesus first demonstrated the power available through His death on the cross. The greatest display of human power ever on the earth was the resurrection of Jesus Christ. No other demonstration of might and victory can come near to that which Jesus displayed in Jerusalem the third day after He was crucified. He defeated death and the grave.

Now, the passion reference of Acts 1:3 refers to the suffering that Christ endured at the crucifixion. But other definitions for *passion* include "strong feeling," "an abandoned display of emotion," "boundless enthusiasm," and "love." I believe these words apply to Acts 1:3 as well. Because of the pain Christ endured on the cross, we can see His "passion of love" for us. The cross was the "love chamber" of the New Testament. It is where He gave His body to His bride and He said, "I was wounded for your transgressions." (See Isaiah 53:5.)

The reason for the passion of Christ was His passion for you and me. His death was a demonstration of the unconditional love He has for us. His focus was on us, and that passion is what ultimately led to the power of the cross. This is the power that you and I have access to. It is power for salvation, healing, provisions, relationships, guidance, and so much more.

Elijah—a man of fervor

If ever there was a man of passion and power, it was Elijah, also know as Elias. We don't know much about Elijah's background. Scripture does not say who his parents were or where he came from. However, we do know that James, the brother of Jesus, said Elijah was "a man subject to like passions" (James 5:17), who saw results. Elijah was passionate about his faith, about his God, and about the power available to believers. Like the early followers of Christ, Elijah's passion never failed to bring results. "Elias was a man subject to like passions as we are, and he prayed earnestly that it might not rain: and it rained not on the earth by the space of three years and six months. And he prayed again, and the heaven gave rain, and the earth brought forth her fruit" (James 5:17–18).

Passion produces power! The Bible says that this prophet had so much power with God that he prayed both drought and fire down from heaven (1 Kings 17–18). Elijah's passion produced power to revive a dead boy (1 Kings 17:22), to outrun a chariot (1 Kings 18:46), and to part water (2 Kings 2:8). He was even fed by angels (1 Kings 19:5). Then, rather than leaving this world in the traditional manner, he "went up by a whirlwind into heaven" on a chariot of fire (2 Kings 2:11). Now, that is what I call power. And power always follows passion.

Elijah said, "I have been very zealous for the LORD God of hosts" (1 Kings 19:10, NKJV). He had emotional, boundless enthusiasm for his God. You cannot be passive or stoic about your faith and experience a manifestation of His resurrection power in your life. God is looking for people who crave His power and who will not be inhibited or afraid to use it.

In chapter 4 of his book *Why Revival Tarries*, evangelist Leonard Ravenhill asks the often-repeated question, "Where are the Elijahs of God?" We cry out to God, "O God, where is Your power? I wish You would give us Elijah's power." You know what I heard God say to me once? He said, "If I could find a man who would come after Me with passion like Elijah, I would release the power of Elijah on that man."

A woman with determination

In chapter 5 of the Book of Mark (the story is also in Matthew 9 and Luke 8), the woman with the issue of blood had such passion and determination that she overcame what seemed to be illogical. Logic said, "There are too many people around Jesus. You cannot get through that crowd." Logic said, "You are ceremonially unclean and cannot go near Christ."

But her passion said, "No matter what my situation, I can get to Jesus. And no matter what my need, He will make it right."

Yes, there were challenges and obstacles to overcome, but this woman wanted her healing more than anything. Mere obstacles would not stand between her and her vision. She had an unrelenting determination—a passionate focus on Jesus Christ.

> A woman in the crowd had suffered for twelve years with constant bleeding. She had suffered a great deal from many doctors, and over the years she had spent everything she had to pay them, but she had gotten no better. In fact, she had gotten worse. She had heard about Jesus, so she came up behind him through the crowd and touched his robe. For she thought to herself, "If I can just touch his robe, I will be healed."
>
> —MARK 5:25–28, NLT

She had suffered enough, and she pushed persistently through the crowd to get her healing. She overcame past failures and pressures. The situation wasn't perfect, but she had only one chance. How passionate was her effort? How badly did she want her healing? Badly enough to pursue it with all that was in her. "Immediately the bleeding stopped, and she could feel in her body that she had been healed of her terrible condition" (Mark 5:29, NLT).

Now up to this point, no one had ever been healed through merely touching Jesus's clothes, but passion produces faith, and faith produces power. You see, the crowd was pressing in on Him, and many were touching Him. Before this woman, no one had touched Him with such passion. Her passion led to a release of Christ's power. "Jesus realized at once that healing power had gone out from him, so he turned around in the crowd and asked, 'Who touched my robe?'" (Mark 5:30, NLT).

The indiscriminate, casual worshiper who touches Christ will not receive His power. You have to have a passionate determination to see your need met. You won't stumble into your healing; you have to pursue it.

And here's a bonus effect. If you look in Matthew 14, you will see that this woman opened up a new spiritual dimension of possibilities for others because of her faith. After she had received her miraculous healing, do you know what the woman did? By using her passion, she broke into a whole new dimension of the anointing through the Spirit of God, an anointing that people did not realize existed. And once she broke through with her passion, others began to get their breakthroughs, using the dimension that she opened up.

Because of one woman who had passion, others got it too. "Soon people were bringing all their sick to be healed. They begged him to let the sick touch at least the fringe of his robe, and all who touched him were healed" (Matt. 14:35–36, NLT).

Today, we keep waiting too long, and then we simply do what everybody else in the body of Christ does—limiting God to what He has done in the past. God wants to open up new dimensions of worship, new dimensions of power for believers. But He must have people with passionate determination who can release this power.

Your turn to change the world

Just as God chose His twelve disciples, He is choosing you today. He is calling you to change the world through the passion and purpose He has placed within you. Get hold of that passion and nothing will be impossible. Your faith can move your mountain (Matt. 17:20; 1 Cor. 13:2), but your fear can create one.

Out of billions of people, Jesus chose twelve men to be the building blocks of the kingdom of God on Earth. It's really an amazing thing. He did not choose them because of what they were to start with. He chose them because of what He knew they could become through His mighty power infused with their passion. God wants us to be passionate about our needs, but He also wants us to be *com*passionate about others. He has given us a mission to go out into the world to share His hope and love.

Your faith can move your mountain,
but your fear can create one.

The disciples were in the Upper Room for ten days, praying, and nothing happened. Sometimes you go through seasons when you're living in the land of nothing and the only thing that will get you through that nothing is passion.

When you are down to nothing, God is up to something!

When Elijah was believing for rain, six times he sent his servant to see what was coming on the horizon. Each time he would ask, "Are there any clouds?" Six times his servant's answer was, "Nothing."

On that seventh trip to check for clouds, Elijah's servant saw a cloud on the horizon. Elijah's miracle was on its way! "And it came to pass in the mean while, that the heaven was black with clouds and wind, and there was a great rain" (1 Kings 18:45).

For twelve years, the woman with the issue of blood sought her healing and saw no results. Then, she received her miraculous healing instantly—it only took one touch.

Don't be afraid of failure. Keep your fire of passion burning deep inside. Don't water down your passion based on the circumstances around you. The disciples were persistent and were rewarded with the power of the Holy Spirit. Keep your faith and you will see that "what things soever ye *desire*, when ye pray, believe that ye receive them, and ye shall have them" (Mark 11:24, emphasis mine). Desire, passion, and power—they belong together.

When you pursue your God-given purpose with a passion, He will anoint you with the power to fulfill it. God's Word is your shield of protection against demons and devils. God's Word is your sword of the spirit that drives the enemy back. You need to be passionate and desire His Word more than you desire money; desire it more than you desire pleasure; desire it more than you desire anything. I want to encourage you today to pray for guidance, seek God's will for your life, and study His Word. Your passion will grow and give you the tools you need to accomplish your God-given purpose. Ask for guidance, seek God's will, study His Word, and your passion and your power will grow.

Passionate people are willing to take risks and try new things. Just consider the way each of the disciples passionately followed the teaching of the Master—even unto death.

Matthew was martyred in Ethiopia. He was slain with an axe. Philip was scourged, imprisoned, and crucified. Thaddaeus died on a cross at Odessa. James the Lesser was stoned and beaten to death with a fuller's club. Thomas was speared because he enraged a pagan priest. John the Beloved was forced into a pot of boiling oil. He miraculously escaped and was exiled to Patmos, where he wrote the Book of Revelation. Peter was slain by Nero upside down on a cross, and his wife was crucified with him. Andrew was crucified on an X-shaped cross. King Herod beheaded James the Elder for his faith in Jesus. Nathanael was tortured and crucified with his head facing downward.

Yes, they met with shocking deaths, but they did something incredible with their lives because of the passion that burned within them. These were the men who "turned the world upside down" and made a way for you and me to hear and respond to the gospel message.

God is looking for people who won't lose their passion no matter what the trial or circumstance. Where is your passion? Where is your compassion? God's presence in your life is a holy thing, a miraculous thing. Your relationship with your heavenly Father should be one of passion and fervor. He should be your focus, your desire, the overwhelming love of your life. If you remember this key, you will never lack His power.

When you are down to nothing,
God is up to something!

This power, born of passion, is what God will use to unleash your divine destiny. You have a God-given purpose, a calling on your life. The passion deep inside you is waiting to be released. God has made a provision of power for you to move forward to achieve that mission. Just tap into the passion of your heart, and remember that passion produces power!

Passion costs you something. It costs to love, it costs to feel, it costs to care, and when Christ hung on that cross, He was saying, "When you look at the cross, don't just see pain, but see My passion for you, My bride." And my prayer is that as He gave His body for you, you would give your body back to Him as a living sacrifice, holy and acceptable to God.

REVIEW

Unfolding Your Dream

- Unfolding your dream starts with *desire*. Desire enables you to persist, even when your circumstances get difficult.

- Besides desire, you need passion. Find your passion and follow it. Remember, power follows passion.

- When you are down to nothing, God is up to something!

- If you follow the example of Jesus, Elijah, the twelve disciples, and many others who have gone before you, you too can be a world changer.

Chapter 6

MAKING ASSETS OF YOUR LIABILITIES

ALL HIS LIFE, ZACCHAEUS HAD TO HEAR those stupid "short" jokes. ("He's so short that...when he sits on the curb, his feet don't touch the street...they can see his feet on his driver's license picture...he has to cuff his underwear.) "Zacchaeus" was too long a name for him, so he had all those short nicknames: Peanut, Squirt, Pipsqueak, Kid, Junior, Sprout, Peewee, Midget, Short Stack—Old Zack always got the short end of the stick.

Zacchaeus's liability was that he was short, and it gave him somewhat of an attitude. To compensate for his lack, he became a tax collector. At last, for a change, folks would have to listen to him. Still, when he couldn't reach things, he had to get a ladder. He had to bring a box or a stepstool to stand on.

When he heard that Jesus was at the edge of town, he wanted a chance to see Him. Jesus would be walking through town on the main street. People were swarming into the street. But Zack knew that if he just walked out there, he'd only see the backs of the people in front of him. So, he got an idea. He climbed a sycamore tree. He tucked his stocky legs under him on a limb, and he waited for Jesus to get closer. All he wanted to do was see Him. He had heard people talking about this guy Jesus, and he wanted to take a look for himself.

He didn't expect Jesus to notice him. Out of the hundreds and hundreds of people who lined the streets that day, Jesus chose *him* to speak to directly. He looked right at him and said, "Zacchaeus, make haste and come down, for today I must stay at your house" (Luke 19:5, NKJV). Zacchaeus's whole life changed. He had met his Savior face-to-face.

It happened *because of*, not in spite of, his liability. If he hadn't been so short, he wouldn't have climbed that tree.

Liabilities become launching pads.

What is your greatest liability? Whatever you have as a liability could turn out to be your greatest asset if it drives you "up a tree" and causes you to see Jesus. If your liability makes you desperate, it can make you willing to do what others aren't willing to do. It can make you ignore what other people think. You can undertake extreme measures to see Him—and if you're that interested in seeing Jesus, you will see Him not only at a distance, but also up close. He will invite Himself to your house. It will change your life.

"You don't understand, Jentezen. I didn't have a good father. My father abandoned the family. I dread Father's Day. I can't stand to even think about my father." But if your lack drives you crazy, it could drive you right into the arms of the best Father in the universe, who will more than make up for your earthly father's absence.

Whatever you have as a liability could turn out to be your greatest asset.

"But Jentezen, I'm not rich like Zacchaeus was. In fact, I'm in a real mess. I lost my job. My unemployment compensation isn't anywhere near enough to pay the bills. My options have dried up..." If your financial liability causes you to climb up higher—pray more, fast, and get yourself squared away with God—then it's worth it.

When I was a teenager, I got really sick. A disease attacked my blood system, and my weight dropped to around one hundred twenty pounds. My waist measured twenty-eight inches. Those were some of the darkest days of my life. I was dragged out of normal teenage living. I couldn't run out on a Friday night with my friends. I couldn't go out at all. I couldn't even go to school.

I went through the dark season for over a year, and it eventually started driving me up a tree. I started to seek God. I kept saying, "God, when are You going to heal me? When is this going to be over?" And He would say nothing—nothing but silence. So I began to devour the Bible. I read the Word all day long. Twenty, thirty, forty chapters a day.

I learned a lot about Him. Out of a dark season like that, you learn things you cannot learn unless you're a "tree person." You learn things you would never learn if your life had been normal and average.

One of the main things I learned was that if God trusts you with a severe trial, a dark season, it's only because He wants to invite Himself to your house. He has something for you that will come right out of your bad situation. Your greatest liability, the thing that makes you shake your fist at heaven and say, "Why? Why?" could become the intimacy point between you and Jesus. You could get connected to wholeness. Your life could turn out a lot better than you ever thought.

In the previous chapter, I mentioned the woman with the issue of blood. Her liability was a major one. In those days, people shunned somebody like her as "unclean." That meant she had been shunned for twelve long years, more than a decade. Is that fair? I don't know. But it made her so desperate that she dared to go right out in the midst of the people who were flocking around Jesus. She didn't climb a tree—she rammed and shoved and pushed her way through the press of bodies in the crowd until she got right up to Him. Then, without a word, she dropped to her knees and touched the hem of His garment. She was thinking, "Out of all these people, it's going to be me." She didn't care what anybody else thought of her right then. She had served her time. She had come to the One who could change everything. She *had* to connect with Jesus.

What if she'd never had the problem in the first place? Do you think she would have developed so much faith and fearlessness? Of course she wouldn't have. She would have missed Jesus too.

Sometimes you have to go through seasons when you're living in "God's nothing." It's so you will seek Him with passionate desperation. Look how it was for the believers in the Upper Room. Jesus had ascended, but the Holy Spirit had not yet come. Day after day they prayed. Nothing. Look how it was for Elijah's servant. Six times he had to run out to see if a cloud might be coming on the horizon. It hadn't rained for three years. What was coming on the horizon? Six times his answer was, "Nothing." Have you ever had to live through the nothings of God?

You see, when you're down to nothing, God really is up to something!

The woman with the issue of blood had used up all of her means on doctors. They couldn't help her. Nothing worked. All Peter had was a worm and a fishhook—and his tax bill was due. He had nothing in his pocketbook. When you're down to nothing, you have to know that God is up to something.

Your problem is the key to your promotion.

Your problem—that thing that is so hard for you right now—is the key to your promotion. Did you know that? Do you believe it? "Your problem is the key to your promotion" is not just a cute little phrase. Look at David and Goliath. Without Goliath, we would never have heard of David. David could have just continued tending sheep out in the fields if God hadn't sent Goliath. In order to become King David, he had to face Goliath. His problem (Goliath) was the key to his promotion (becoming king).

When David faced down Goliath, he did it with true confidence. Awhile back, when I was getting ready to preach about David and Goliath, I read the story through from beginning to end, and I noticed something I had never seen before: David never called Goliath a "giant." His brothers did, and so did the other Israelite troops. The Philistines did too. King Saul probably did. But not David. Never. The only name David called him was "you uncircumcised Philistine." This focused on the fact that Goliath was an "un-covenant man," because circumcision was the mark of the Old Testament covenant between God and the Israelites.

So, by labeling him an "uncircumcised Philistine," David was declaring him to be much smaller than God, who was the *true* giant in the situation.

Can you figure out what your Goliath is? What's your biggest obstacle or problem? It may just be the key to your promotion. In order for you to step into your destiny, you will need to face down your Goliath-sized problem in God's unbeatable strength. Believing that you can do it is more than half of your battle.

Successful failures

I've been paying attention to successful people for years, and one thing I've noticed is that many, many of them are what could be called "successful failures." What I mean by that is that they suffered crushing blows and failures before they ever managed to become a success.

Truett Cathy is a good example. He's the man who founded the Chick-fil-A restaurant chain, which started with one small diner and has grown to more than one thousand restaurants, making it the second-largest quick-service chicken restaurant chain in the nation.[1]

As of the September 2007 *Forbes* listing of billionaires, Cathy was number 380 in the United States, with a net worth of 1.3 billion dollars.[2] And this was achieved while remaining closed on Sundays, which is one of the busiest sales days of the week.

Mr. Cathy has written several books, and in his autobiography, he revealed that he was so tongue-tied that he couldn't put three words together verbally without stumbling over himself. Three weeks after he opened his first store, it burned to the ground. When he finally got his second store built, his brothers, who were his partners, were all killed in an airplane crash.[3]

Doesn't that sound like a prize-winning recipe for failure? I'm sure there were negative voices who advised him to quit. "Just give up, man! What's the use? Why keep trying?" But he kept trying, and today there's a tremendous business that has employed thousands and fed millions!

His challenges and near failures were not too much of a handicap for Truett Cathy. In fact, they may have been his best motivation.

The lepers' liabilities

Do you see how important our liabilities can be? Without them, most of us would just settle for the status quo. We'd never exert ourselves to move up to grab hold of God's provision for our lives.

It reminds me of another story in the Bible, the story of the four lepers who lived outside the city wall at Samaria. (See 2 Kings 6:24–7:20.) They had to live on the outside of the walls because they were contaminated and contagious with leprosy. People would throw food scraps over the wall to those four guys, and they would eat the scraps while sitting in the dirt. (Sometimes I think they were like a lot of people in the church, so content with scraps that they don't consider seeking for better fare.) I believe those lepers would have sat there for *years*, content with the scraps, if they hadn't been thrown into a major crisis.

The king of Syria besieged the city, and the people began to starve to death. Needless to say, no more scraps came over the wall for the poor lepers. They just sat there and listened to their stomachs growl. The famine got so bad, the Bible says, that people inside the city started eating donkey's heads and dove's dung and even boiling their own children.

Finally, the lepers were so desperate that they decided to go into the enemy's camp. If they got killed, what difference would it make? They were going to die anyway (2 Kings 7:3–4).

See, a famine will help you make a "destiny decision." It was time for them to move out. They needed to be motivated to leave behind the land of famine and walk into the place of plenty. A famine made these lepers get up and walk toward the place where they knew there was food. They walked by faith.

And when they got to the edge of the camp, what did they find? Nobody. Those Syrians had thought they heard the sound of an army coming. They had left everything—food, clothing, everything—and they had fled.

Those lepers expected to face a barrage of arrows, but instead the bigger foe turned out to be the fear inside them. It's the same with you and me. The circumstances have never been our real problem. God is always greater than anything out there. The real problem has always been the battles inside our own minds and hearts. You know from experience that that's the truth. That's why you must believe that you can.

It didn't take long before they realized that they should tell the starving people inside the city that the siege was over. So they changed out of their beggar's rags into some of the nice clothes they found in the tents, and they began to load up wagons with food and valuables. It was a miracle. The city was saved. And it would not have happened if the lepers' liability had not driven them to take a big risk. Their liability had become their greatest asset.

Worship on the partial.

Most of the time, our liabilities aren't physical ones. Even when we have a physical problem like the lepers did, sometimes it seems like our biggest two liabilities are lack of faith and lack of perseverance. It can sometimes take years before we see results. We need to hold on to our vision through all sorts of setbacks, and we need to believe that our God is more than able to carry us through. He will every time, if we hang on to Him.

One of the best ways to hang on to God is by worshiping and praising Him, regardless of what your circumstances look like. When Zerubbabel and Nehemiah returned from Babylon to Jerusalem to rebuild the walls of Jerusalem, they started, of course, with the foundation. It was hard, hard work, clearing rubble and moving massive slabs of rock. On top of that, their enemies were opposed to their return. Each day was difficult, but each day counted, because they'd get a little more done. (See Nehemiah 7.)

We need to hold on to our vision
through all sorts of setbacks.

After a while, they finished the foundation. They hadn't yet built the walls. They hadn't yet set up the curtains and the gold and the altars. They had laid only the foundation. You know what a foundation looks like: it's just the shape of the future building, and there's still a lot of work to do.

At that point, the people took a break. And what did they do? The Book of Ezra says this:

> When the builders laid the foundation of the temple of the LORD, they set the priests in their apparel with trumpets, and the Levites the sons of Asaph with cymbals, to praise the LORD, after the ordinance of David king of Israel. And they sang together by course in praising and giving thanks unto the LORD; because he is good, for his mercy endureth for ever toward Israel. And all the people shouted with a great shout, when they praised the LORD, because the foundation of the house of the LORD was laid.
>
> —Ezra 3:10–11

The people made so much noise shouting and worshiping that the noise could be heard "afar off" (Ezra 3:13). Why so much worship so early in the rebuilding process? It didn't look like much yet. The times were unstable and insecure, and anything could happen to interrupt the ongoing work. Wasn't it a little premature to start a worship service?

No, not at all. The worship itself probably helped the work to proceed successfully. You see, they were worshiping "on the partial." In faith, they were seeing the completed temple. They were praising God for what they had achieved already and putting their trust in Him that it would be completed as planned.

If you can learn to worship "on the partial"—when you don't yet have it all; you don't have everything to fulfill your ultimate dream; you haven't yet "seen the walls go up"—you will have learned how to walk your vision through to completion. You will be expressing your faith in a God who is able to see you through to the end. When God starts something, He always finishes it. That's something to praise Him for! Worship *cannot* wait.

Many of us think we have to wait for our complete victory to happen before we can open our mouths and our hearts in full worship. But I'm telling you that one way to stir up your faith and joy and energy is to begin to worship on the partial. The deal is this: "The joy of the LORD is your strength" (Neh. 8:10). If you lose your joy, then you lose your strength. If you lose your strength, you lose your power to resist the enemy. If you lose the power to resist the enemy, he will have you for lunch.

But if you can worship God, even when all you have in front of you are the foundation stones, the joy of the Lord will fill your heart, and you will not find it so difficult to resist the enemy. "Resist the devil, and he will flee from you" (James 4:7). If you feel that your faith is getting low, help it out by boosting your joy. The enemy wants you to get depressed. Satan wants you to throw in the towel. The devil wants you to fall into depression, worry, and negative thinking.

The antidote is simple—it's worship and praise. Ask yourself the question: Is my God able? Of course, you know the answer. He's able to finish what He starts, and He's able to keep you in there. He's not going to leave you where you are. He's not going to back up and abandon you now. He's not going to say, "You're on your own from here on." God doesn't do that. Anything He starts, you can count on Him to finish. So, praise Him when the fulfillment of your vision is only partial. It's a start—you're already moving toward the finish line!

Praise God *all* the time.

Some time ago, I read about a ten-year study of dozens of families, and it was determined that nearly 90 percent of the time, something was wrong with their marriages or kids or finances or something. That appeared to be typical.

That means that if you are one of those people who can only praise God when things are going right, then you're going to limit your praise to about 10 percent of your whole life. You won't worship God when things get a little crazy. Don't be that kind of person. You'll wait too long between perfect stretches.

If you worship on the partial, you will be able to worship all the time, and that is the best way to stay close to Him.

The Four Horns

In the Bible, horns are a symbol or a type of power. In the Book of Zechariah, there is a prophetic word about four horns. (See Zechariah 1:17–21.) These four horns represented four powerful nations that came against the city of Jerusalem right after God had promised prosperity and comfort to the people so they could "spread abroad" His goodness. As soon as God decreed prosperity, these four horns of resistance rose up to hold down God's people.

God has decreed a word over you. He has spoken prosperity over you. I'm talking about prospering in the dream that God has given you to spread it further, to do more, and to enlarge your territory. But that doesn't mean that horns will not come to resist the prosperity of God from breaking forth and spreading abroad in your life.

Zechariah also saw four carpenters. These four carpenters were coming to build up what the four horns would tear down. Jesus was the Son of a carpenter, and Paul said, "I am a master builder." Just when the horns of the enemy come to press you down and defeat you, God will send the Spirit of the Carpenter to build you back up, to lift you up, to encourage you, and to tell you, "The joy of the Lord is your strength."

These four horns don't have names in the Bible, but I have given them names, picking out four ways that Satan tries to hold down God's people. I have called them the horn of lack, the horn of limitation, the horn of hindrance, and the devouring horn.

The horn of lack

The first horn represents lack. The horn of lack says, "This is the level that you will operate on for the rest of your life. You're stuck here."

You can get used to a life of lack, but as soon as you start to lift your head up and say, "I'm going to rise to another level so I can do more for God and for my family and for the kingdom," that horn of lack will show up and try to keep you in the same territory that you're used to. Sometimes, "lack" has been keeping you down for so long, even for generations, that you don't realize what it is. You can grow accustomed to a lack of joy, a lack of love in your marriage, a lack of confidence, a lack of peace, or a lack of finances. The horn of lack tries to convince you that God will bless some but He'll never bless you. Are you having a lack attack? The horn of lack tells you, "Just keep your head down and stay oppressed, defeated, depressed, and barely getting by."

It's what I call "settling for the duct-tape level." Why do I say that? Because you just keep putting duct tape on everything to hold it together. It doesn't even cross your mind to believe God for something better.

It's like our television ministry used to be. For many years, it was a struggle. God had provided our first cameras, but ten years later, they were falling to pieces. One day I walked into the studios and saw all this old equipment. There was duct tape on everything I saw. It would have been funny if it hadn't been so sad. The cameras had duct tape holding the lenses on. Cords were held together with duct tape. The studio lights were held in position with duct tape. The recorders were duct-taped together in stacks. There was duct tape here, duct tape there, here a little duct tape, there a little duct tape. The television director just carried around a big roll of duct tape. Right there, the Lord spoke to me and said, "That's the kind of faith you have—duct-tape faith." And as I looked around, He added, "You know why you're at duct-tape level? It's because you can't believe Me for anything better than this."

At that time, we were building a new sanctuary, and it was just a shell of a building. I told them to get the cameras and bring them to the empty sanctuary. I stood on a box in the middle of the sanctuary and told the television crew, "We've got duct tape all over everything. God just told me that He wants to take the duct tape off our television ministry." We made a declaration of what God had said. The horn of lack wanted me to accept things the way they were; its assignment was to convince me that it would never be any better.

Within thirty days, 1.3 million dollars came in, and we bought the latest equipment that money could buy. Since then, our television ministry has never been in a season like that. Since then, we've always had more than enough, overflow, reserves. The Spirit of the Carpenter came to turn our liabilities into assets.

In your own life, has a spirit of lack dug itself into you like the point of a horn? Why don't you just say this: "In the name of Jesus, you horn of lack, you are not legal in my life. I serve a God of super-abundance. I serve a God who says, 'You shall have good success' (Josh. 1:8) and 'Whatever your hand touches, it will prosper' (Gen. 39; 2 Chron. 20:20). I'm not going to listen to the negative voices anymore." Say good-bye to the duct-tape level forever!

The horn of limitation

The second horn is called the horn of limitation. The horn of limitation is different from the horn of lack. When you are being held down by the horn of limitation, you know that the power and the blessings of God are real. You know that miracles are real, healing is real, and prosperity exists. But you think, "It's not for me." You're limited. The horn of limitation puts a ceiling over you. It tells you that you can succeed to a certain degree, but then you will peak and you won't be able to go any higher.

The horn of limitation makes you feel like one of the trained elephants I saw on a *National Geographic* special. The elephant trainer had a massive bull elephant with huge tusks, and he was held by a rope—not a chain, but a little rope. The rope was attached to a little cement block that the elephant could have just picked up if he had wanted to. But every time the elephant walked a little bit and felt the tug of the rope, he stopped. Why was that? Why didn't that powerful elephant just go wherever he wanted to, like on those *Elephants Gone Wild* videos, where they escape and go running through the streets, trampling on cars?

Here's what the trainer said: "Well, we get an elephant when it's young. We tie a chain around its leg and the chain is connected to a cement block that's buried in the earth. Young as he is, there's no way he can break the chain or move the block. At first he will try to break free. But he can't do it. Finally, always, inevitably, the moment comes when his mind accepts that this is as far as he will ever be able to go. Even when the elephant gets as big as that bull and he's not the same elephant that he used to be, he doesn't recognize that he has the strength to move farther than the limits of his rope."

In the elephant's mind, a limitation has been established. It tells him, "You can go this far and no farther." Too often that is what has happened to us. We have had limitations imposed on us. We accept them, and we believe them, even when we have long since "outgrown" them.

If you are not careful, the horn of limitation will get a hold of your life, and suddenly you will begin to accept those limitations. You must determine to push down those limitations. Hear the voice of the Holy Spirit calling you to go a little further, do a little more. Use your faith, and expand beyond the limitations.

Because the elephant has accepted the limitations in his mind, he fails to see that he isn't the same young elephant he used to be. He has grown; he is mightier and stronger. I want to say to you, "You're not the same person you used to be." Tell yourself that you're not the person you used to be and that your old limits don't apply to you anymore. When Jesus came into your heart, were you anchored to an addiction? Maybe you were chained to failure. Maybe nobody in your family has ever had a successful marriage, so you feel the tug of that limitation. Perhaps no one in your family has earned a college degree or has achieved financial success, so you think you won't either.

The Spirit of the Carpenter wants to begin to build you up in your confidence and faith enough to make you free from the limitations that have held you back. Let the Carpenter come and show you how free and strong you really are. Let Him break off your limitations. When He does that for you, it may help other people do the same thing.

In 1954, a runner named Roger Bannister broke the four-minute mile. Up to that point, nobody had ever done it before; they had said it was humanly impossible. Interestingly, in the year after he did it, thirty people broke the same record. The year after that, more than three hundred people ran the mile in less than four minutes. The hardest thing was breaking through that artificial limit the first time. When people could imagine doing it, they did it.

The first time is always the hardest. I still remember the feeling I had the first time I raised my hand in worship. I don't think anything about raising my hands now, but the first time, I had an insecure feeling. I remember the first time I gave one thousand dollars away. That amount of money is some kind of a barrier. You can see it on people. You can tell when they're in the middle of breaking free of a limitation on their giving, especially if they are bringing their gift down the aisle of the church. They look like dead men walking. But once they do it, they're free to do it again, and the next time is a lot easier.

The enemy wants you to stay in your limitation. He wants you to put your head down and go into a foxhole because your life is difficult. Just tell that spirit of limitation, "Spirit of limitation, you're not going to hold me down. I'm getting up right now." And then talk success and freedom to yourself. Choose your words wisely. Don't reinforce those old limitations anymore. Death and life are in the power of the tongue. When you go to the doctor, one of the first things the doctor will say is, "Stick out your tongue." Why? He can see if you're sick by examining your tongue. God also says, "Stick out your tongue. Let Me check out what you've been saying." If you ever break free from the horn of limitation and declare, "I believe that I can," then, and only then, you will!

The horn of hindrance

In the Book of 1 Thessalonians, Paul named the evil spirit of the third horn. "I desire to come to you, but Satan has *hindered* me." (See 1 Thessalonians 2:18.)

This hindering spirit gets in front of you and blocks you. It keeps you from making progress. It jabs you and hits you, trying to slow you down and trip you up. It sees that you are still moving in spite of the horn of lack and the horn of limitation, and it tries to throw up a roadblock to hinder your journey.

But in the Spirit of the Carpenter you can say, "Horn of hindrance, you can buffet me. You can try to hinder me. You can delay me. But you cannot destroy me. And you can't stop me. You can knock me down, but 'the righteous will get up seven times.'" (See Proverbs 24:16.)

Let the Carpenter hammer on the third horn until it no longer hinders you.

The devouring horn

Now, after you've prevailed against the resistance that gets in front of you to try to hinder you and limit you, another one will get behind you. This one appears in Malachi 3:11—the devouring horn.

This horn chases after you and runs you down like a lion chasing his prey. When you think you've finally gotten your breakthrough and you are starting to see some victories in the harvest, if you don't watch out, this devouring horn will begin to steal the fruitfulness that God has given you.

At first, you may not know what's going on. But when you realize what's happening, you can bind that horn up just like you did the other ones in the authority and strength of the Spirit of the Carpenter.

It doesn't matter if people try to block your path. It doesn't matter if your circumstances look hopeless. The Spirit of God wants you to reach your destiny, and He will help you turn what seems like liabilities into assets every time.

I am an asset owner.

My dad never pastored big churches. So to me, when my church hit seven hundred members, that was really big. But we stayed at about seven hundred members for a long time. I think it was because I was being hindered by spirits of limitation and lack.

I already mentioned "duct-tape faith." When I told a national television audience that our cameras were held together with duct tape, a seventy-three-year-old woman sent me something in the mail. It was a donation, but it was a different kind of donation. She sent me a one-thousand-dollar bill. I had never seen one before.

This lady sent a letter with the money. She wrote, "God told me to send you a one-thousand-dollar bill as a memorial to remind you. He said you can use it if you want to, but don't use it unless you have to. Put it somewhere so it can be a memorial to you that

God has at least one thousand more people out there who will send one thousand dollars each to pay for your new TV equipment." You know what? I have never had to use it.

It has helped me make a positive confession, and that has kept me ahead of the horns that cause lack, limitation, hindrance, and devouring.

Here's how a positive confession sounds: "In Jesus's name, you horns of lack, limitation, hindrance, and devouring are defeated. By the Spirit of the Carpenter, Jesus Christ, you are struck down. Spirit of lack and spirit of limitation, you will not hold me at the same level anymore. I'm going to where I've never been before. You hindering spirit that is in front of me, jabbing me and tripping me and slowing me down, you must get out of my way, in Jesus's name. You devouring spirit that keeps coming up behind me, trying to steal what God has given me, in Jesus's name you are rebuked.

"I am an asset owner. I am a land possessor. I am a kingdom builder. I am a wise investor. I am blessed, blessed, blessed. All of my liabilities have been turned into assets. Amen."

You may need to pray like this more than once. Why does it seem to take so long sometimes? I believe God sometimes holds off on answering our prayers quickly because our faith grows so much between the time we ask God to come and the time He actually does.

When Daniel was thrown into the den of lions, I believe that Daniel's faith grew, not just up to when they threw him in, but also when he saw the lions' mouths coming at him with their sharp teeth, and up to that very moment when the angel of God shut them down. Then he could stay there, secure and confident. The next morning, the king gave orders for the den to be opened so that Daniel's body (he assumed) could be taken out. Lo and behold, "Daniel was taken up out of the den and no injury whatever was found on him, because he had trusted in his God" (Dan. 6:23, NASU).

Daniel proved what you and I can also prove—that God is never too late. When He shows up, what appeared to be an impossible situation will suddenly turn into a victory.

Right now, as quickly as you can, open your mouth and confess that God is able to save you; He's able to bring you through in one piece; He's able to do far more abundantly than all you can ask or think (Eph. 3:20).

Worship Him. Let your faith rise. Turn those liabilities of yours into *assets*, and "press on toward the goal for the prize of the upward call of God in Christ Jesus" (Phil. 3:14, NASU).

REVIEW

Making Your Liabilities Into Assets

- Your seemingly insurmountable problems can become launching platforms for your faith.

- Sometimes you must go through seasons when you're living in "God's nothing" so you will seek Him with passionate desperation.

- Make a positive confession. Open your mouth with praise; confess that your God is able. He is!

- With God's help, you can prevail over the "four horns" that will try to tear you down: the spirit of lack, the spirit of limitation, the spirit of hindrance, and the devouring spirit.

Chapter 7

LIVING IN THE FAITH ZONE

CHUCK YEAGER WAS THE WORLD WAR II hero who first broke the sound barrier. Everybody who had tried it before had gotten to a certain speed, and the plane had started to shake so violently that it seemed as if the plane would disintegrate. Some planes did disintegrate, and the pilots died. In other words, experience showed that it couldn't be done. But Yeager wanted to try anyway. He was twenty-four years old.

Right before he was supposed to try it in October of 1947, he cracked two of his left ribs in a horseback-riding accident. He was in extreme pain. People told him he shouldn't go up. He wondered if his body was capable of performing well enough under the stress. But he got into the plane and did it. He said, "At seven hundred miles an hour, the plane began to rattle and shake violently." But then he broke through into "a great calm." He'd done it.

That's how it is when you're about to get a breakthrough. Everything around you starts shaking and falling apart. Everything goes crazy. You might be in pain. You feel as if your whole world is falling to pieces. But that's not an indication that you're going to crash. As if God would drop something He had started! As if He would let you crash and burn!

Like Chuck Yeager, we need to find a way to break through our difficulties into the next level of victory.

Breakout comes before breakthrough.

If you're in a shaking situation, you are just on the other side of a great calm. The key to breaking through is to break out and go for it. You have to say, "I don't care what history says. I don't care what people say. I know God has given me a promise."

If you do want to break barriers and establish new territory, and if you want your life to make a difference, you need to realize that times of shaking *will* happen. In fact, the worse the shaking times, the more glorious the breakthroughs. But you can't start with the breakthrough. You need to start by breaking out in your own mind and in your own faith. Once you break out and pave the way to the breakthrough, other people can follow you.

If you're in a shaking situation, you are
just on the other side of a great calm.

You may be the one breakout person in your whole family. You may be the only one serving God. Your family may give you a terrible time if you ask them to come to church with you. Well, let them shake, rattle, and roll. All God needs is one breakout person in the family. If He can get—and keep—His breakout person, the breakthroughs will come. It's a guarantee.

The prophet Micah said, "The one who breaks open will come up before them; they will break out, pass through the gate, and go out by it" (Mic. 2:13, NKJV).

What does that mean, "break out"? Break out of what? Break out of self-imposed limitations. Break out of negative thinking. Break out of insecurities. Break out of fears. Break out of past failures. Break out of where you came from and the limitations that were put on you. Break out of depression and hopelessness. Break out of a self-defeating mentality that says, "Nothing's ever going to change in my life." If you break out, then God's breakthrough can happen.

When God's breakthrough happens, it means that Satan's line of defense has been shattered, so the breakthrough has to do with the enemy. But the breakout also has to do with *you*.

Instead of saying, "I need a breakthrough. I need a breakthrough. I need a breakthrough," you need to start saying, "I need a breakout. I need a breakout. I need a breakout." You need to declare, "I'm not going to let these fears torment me. I'm not going to let failure dominate me. I'm not going to let my mistakes and my past be lord over me."

Well-known leadership expert John Maxwell was asked how he became such a success. He answered, quoting Thomas Edison: "I failed my way to success." What he meant was that he learned more from the wrong things that happened in his life than he ever learned from the right things. One of the best things to learn from a seeming failure is to pick yourself up and try again. You break out of what didn't work, and you say to yourself, "Well, now I know what *doesn't* work. Now I can mark that off the list."

Instead of saying, "I need a breakthrough," you need to start saying, "I need a breakout."

The fulfillment of your dreams will not happen overnight. But you don't have to wait forever for a breakthrough. You can stir yourself to break out of whatever mind-set is holding you back.

One against six hundred

The Philistines were the terrorists of the world about three thousand years ago. They were a murderous, aggressive people, and they roamed around killing anybody who got in their way.

There's a story in the Book of Judges about how a farmer named Shamgar saved Israel from destruction by single-handedly killing six hundred Philistines with an oxgoad. (An oxgoad is a seven-foot-long wooden pole with a sharp steel point on the end.)

The Book of Judges mentions Shamgar's name twice, which is pretty amazing, considering that he was a "nobody": "After him came Shamgar the son of Anath, who struck down six hundred Philistines with an oxgoad; and he also saved Israel" (Judg. 3:31, NASU). "In the days of Shamgar the son of Anath, in the days of Jael, the highways were unoccupied, and the travellers walked through byways" (Judg. 5:6).

When Shamgar saw his family and his nation being overtaken by the Philistine's terrorist threats, he probably already had his oxgoad in his hand, because it was the tool he used every working day to keep his oxen moving across his fields. Under the circumstances, that tool was converted into a lethal weapon. Killing six hundred strong men by yourself seems like an impossible feat, and yet Shamgar succeeded.

I see three keys to his success, and I want to list them because you and I need to know about them. Some of us face incredible odds. Our odds may not be six hundred to one, but they're bad enough. For some of us, the odds are physical. You may have been given a medical report that seems impossible to change. You're up against an enemy, and nobody expects you to win against it. Maybe your odds are financial, and you're finding it hard to believe that "with God all things are possible" (Mark 10:27).

I doubt that any of us are facing six hundred assassins, as Shamgar did. Nevertheless, he succeeded when a lesser man would have failed, all because he stepped out on three simple truths:

1. He started where he was.
2. He used what he had.
3. He did what he could.

I realize that these just seem too simple. But, like many simple things, they are profound when you start to look at them.

He started where he was. Where was he? He was a farmer, and he started in his field. The field where he grew his crops became his battlefield.

Shamgar wasn't in the army. He wasn't at war college. He wasn't in a powerful position. I'm sure he wished he were in different circumstances, because his placement was not ideal. He was just a farmer who had a family and neighbors and no protection at all from the Philistines. He realized that if anything was going to change concerning his future, he would have to do something about it personally.

That reminds me of the story of the founder of Domino's Pizza, Tom Monaghan. He started where he was in 1960, with one little, hole-in-the-wall pizza shop. He struggled to make ends meet for eight years. In the eighth year, a fire burned his little shop to ashes, and the insurance company would pay him only one cent on the dollar for his losses. All he knew was pizza, so he started another shop. He had to work one-hundred-hour workweeks, seven days a week, and up to this point, he had only taken one weeklong vacation—for his honeymoon.[1] By 1971 he was in debt to the tune of 1.5 million dollars, which is a lot of money to owe when you don't have any way to pay it back.[2]

So, still occupying his "field," which was the pizza business, he decided to try something radical. He decided to limit his menu to pizza only and to deliver it hot and fresh to customers—for free—instead of expecting them to come in to the store to get their pizzas. His plan worked. It worked so well that many others have imitated his business plan. By 2007, Domino's Pizza franchise had grown to include 6,100 stores across the United States and in numerous other countries.[3] Today, Tom Monaghan is one of the richest men in the country, and he is spending most of his money on philanthropic causes. Monaghan kept getting back up, and he kept trying.

In the New Testament, we read "Be instant [prepared] in season, out of season" (2 Tim. 4:2). We're supposed to be prepared and ready for whatever happens. The word *season* in Greek (*eukairos*) has to do with *opportunity*. In other words, we had better be preparing ourselves now when it looks like nothing is happening, because the season will change and the opportunity to act will appear. When an opportunity comes, you need to be prepared for it. You only get one shot sometimes.

Shamgar used what he had. He didn't have an M1 tank or a Blackhawk helicopter. His resources were extremely limited. All he had was his oxgoad. That thing wasn't meant to be a weapon. But he used it every day for his work, and he was good at handling it.

What's your "oxgoad"? God has given you one. He has provided something that you can use in the situation you're in. It could be something you are already very familiar with. He wants to show you what it is, and He wants you to use it with confidence and strength, taking what you have and applying every ounce of your ability to use it well. I'm sure that Shamgar didn't just slouch out to the field with his oxgoad, muttering to his wife over his shoulder, "Well, darlin', I guess I'll go out there and fight Philistines today. Probably I'm gonna get killed, but here I go." No, I think he must have been pretty intense.

If you're in God and God is in you, you should be brimming with enthusiasm.

119

I think Shamgar was fired up, roaring out to the field. Whether he charged at all six hundred of the Philistines at once or whether he ambushed them, we don't know. I like to think that he picked them off in a narrow place. Maybe he killed "only" thirty or forty at a time, and by the time the few he missed got through, they turned around and saw, instead of the rest of their army, this wild-looking, bloody man with an oxgoad in his hand.

Shamgar used what he had, which was his oxgoad—and his enthusiasm. Did you know that our word *enthusiasm* comes from a Greek root, *entheos*, which means "in God," or even "possessed by a god." If you're in God and God is in you, you should be brimming with enthusiasm. You should be turbocharged about your life. Being fired up was as much of a key ingredient for Shamgar's success as his oxgoad was.

You too can take what you have in your hand and use it. You can be like the little boy in the Gospels who offered his lunch to Jesus and Jesus multiplied it. Give God what you have, and the miracle can happen. The miracle comes from what you already have, not from what you don't have.

That's what Mother Teresa always told people too. After she became successful and famous because of her ministry to the sick and dying street people of Calcutta, India, admirers would pursue her. They would say, "Oh, Mother! I want to do what you do! I want to give up everything I own and join your work!"

She would always have the same four-word reply: "Find your own Calcutta." In other words, she was saying, "Follow your own dream." And she was saying, "Use what you already have."

Henry Ford was once asked "What is your secret of success?" His answer: "When you start something, finish it." He knew what he was talking about because he'd had to persevere through five bankruptcies and some pretty colossal mistakes, like forgetting to put a reverse gear in his first Tin Lizzie.

Shamgar didn't go out there assuming that he would fail. He didn't go out there thinking that he couldn't make a difference. The thought never occurred to him. He just stepped out with what he had and used it until he was done. He persevered. He didn't quit or run away.

Martin Luther King Jr. was another person who used what he could. When he attended Morehouse College in Atlanta, Georgia, his speech professors wrote him a note on top of one of the speeches he had delivered to the class: "Martin, if you continue to use such lofty words and flamboyant language, you will never be very effective in public speaking." I have always wondered if that professor was watching when King stood at the podium and gave his "I have a dream" speech. I hope so. King took his "lofty words and flamboyant language," and he did what he could with them.

Let's do what we can with the resources we already have. We have an extra secret weapon that Shamgar doesn't mention, and that's prayer. With prayer in our arsenal, we can do a lot more than we can without it. Prayer takes us to places we can't go in person. E. M. Bounds said, "Prayers outlive the lives of those who utter them." He also said, "Prayers are deathless. Prayers outlive a generation, outlive an age, outlive a world."

You're only courageous when you do what's right despite your fears!

121

It is impossible to overexaggerate the importance of prayer to the success of everything you do. When Jesus said, "Whatever you ask in My name, I'll do it," He was talking about prayer. (See John 14:13.) All things are possible if you pray. (See Matthew 19:26; Mark 9:23; 10:27; 14:36.)

A word about faith versus fear

You know what they say about fear: FEAR—False Evidence Appearing Real. Fear comes in two categories:

1. Fear that I won't get what I need
2. Fear that I won't be able to hold on to what I have

Anybody who ever beat the odds or made a difference did it in spite of their fear. They did it because they were desperate and felt like they didn't have a choice. Sometimes they were inspired by somebody else's example. They said, "If not me, then who? If not now, when?" They didn't think much about it at all, or else they might have changed their mind.

What are you waiting for—a feeling of courage? Forget it! It doesn't exist. You're only courageous when you do what's right despite your fears!

See if you can figure out what you're afraid of. If you can name it, you can conquer it. And understand this: fear attracts Satan like faith attracts God.

For several years I had traveled as an evangelist, speaking on an average of six nights a week in different churches. During that time, I perfected a basic repertoire of about thirty sermons, which I'd preached so often that had I dropped dead in the middle of any of them, my wife could have finished them. So, when I was asked to become pastor of Free Chapel, I faced the challenge of preparing three new sermons each week. My greatest fear was that I couldn't do it. Did I have what it takes to stay fresh, grow my congregation, and build a strong pulpit ministry? Looking back, I see God's wisdom at work. He placed me in a small community where I could do the least amount of damage while still learning.

Every weekend the challenge came back. By Tuesday the pressure began to build as I approached Sunday. Often I'd study until 2:00 a.m. or 3:00 a.m. on Sunday morning and leave my office feeling drained and apprehensive, praying, "Lord, if You don't help me this morning, I'm sunk!"

But I learned to swim. I became a reader, discovered great resources, developed discipline and solid study habits, and above all, I learned to lean on God as never before.

The Bible is a David-and-Goliath book. It teaches you that with God on your side, you're bigger than any problem. The question is, do you believe that enough to step out and allow God to use you? If you're just believing God for things you can do for yourself, you're limiting Him. Furthermore, if you think He'll never ask you to do things you can't do, think again! Jesus told one man to walk on water and another to come out of his grave—and they did!

I can tell you from my own experience that when you find yourself experiencing things that are beyond your ability, that's when you know God is at work, demonstrating His great power.

Everything big starts with something small. All God needs is something to start with!

Miracles only begin when you take what you have and put it into His hands. The moment you make it available to Him, it will begin to grow. "But I have so many weaknesses," you say. The good news is, you can be strong in certain areas and struggling in others, yet God will still use you. Are the same voices that I heard in my early years of ministry telling you that you'll never make it? Get rid of your life-limiting thoughts! Start dreaming! When God defines you, what difference does anybody else's opinion make?

Stop trying to be what you're not, and discover what you are. Instead of comparing yourself to others, recognize what God has called you to be, accept the gifts He's given you, and start building on them. Everything big starts with something small. All God needs is something to start with!

Living in the Faith Zone

Whatever season you are in, God wants you to learn to say, "I *cannot* do this in my own strength. I need to lean on Him." You'll never have all the answers, so you might as well leave the risk-free "safe zone," where you can figure out the next step and where you can handle whatever comes your way, in favor of living in the faith zone.

As I said earlier, living in the faith zone means reaching up and grabbing hold of nothing and holding on to it until it becomes something. God wants you to live there. In fact, He wants you to live there so much that He will stretch you again and again. (He'll let you stay in your safe zone for a while if you need to, but He really does not want you to *live* there.)

Let Him challenge you.

Let God challenge you to step out on nothing. Even if you're not particularly desperate at the moment, allow yourself to become willing to take a faith risk just because He is calling you.

When you move out into the faith zone, you'll find out that that's where God *lives*.

I would not be writing this to you if I had chosen to live my life in the safe zone. When I had been an evangelist for a while, I was in the safe zone. I was in my denomination. Cherise and I were traveling and ministering. We were doing fine, and we had a dependable salary. We felt that we had a good future and that everything was "up and bright." But right in the midst of that security and everything going right, God's Spirit began to agitate me and stir me up with tremendous discontent.

I found myself absolutely miserable, even though I had everything (I thought). God's Spirit began to touch me, and He said, "Are you ready to move out of the safe zone into the faith zone? You can stay here, and it will be OK, but you'll never get to see the miracles, you'll never get to see the supernatural, you'll never get to see what I really could have done in your life—unless you'll dare to get out of that safe zone and step into the faith zone."

I'm so glad I said yes to His invitation! We went from doing *good* things to being in God's perfect will, and there's a big difference between those two. Now, I need to tell you that if you're in God's perfect will, you may find yourself feeling very unsafe at times. You will feel extremely uncomfortable. But you will learn to depend on the Lord as you never could learn back in the comfort of your safe zone. Remember, when a God-given opportunity comes along, it's God's gift to you. What you do with that opportunity is your gift to God.

You need to understand something about God. The Bible says, "Without faith it is impossible to please him" (Heb. 11:6). That means that it does not matter how much religious activity is going on in your life. If you are not relying on your faith, you are not pleasing God.

> *When a God-given opportunity comes along, it is God's gift to you. What you do with that opportunity is your gift to God.*

If you're in the safe zone, you don't really have to pray and seek God for anything because you feel OK about what you have already. You don't really have to be anointed because you can do everything without the anointing. Even though the security of the safe zone is what we try to achieve our whole life long, it's not God's will for His children. His will is that His children will always be dependent upon Him. Always.

If you want to be where God is, break out of the risk-free safe zone and start living in the faith zone. It's risky, but the faith zone is where God lives!

The faith zone is where miracles happen. You'll never see a "Red Sea" part as long as you stay back in the safe zone. You'll never see manna come supernaturally from heaven. You'll never see the miraculous things God wants to do in your life—the exceedingly, abundantly, above-all-you-can-ask-or-think things—as long as you have it "made in the shade."

You may feel that you've heard this message before, and it didn't work for you. You tried taking a risk, you tried walking on water, and you sank like a stone. Just remember what I said earlier about failure. It's the pathway to success. Look at Moses again. There he was, eighty years old, and he'd already spent forty years in the wilderness, looking after sheep. His life looked like a pretty complete failure. He thought he'd heard God the last time, and look what happened. And then a burning bush strikes up a conversation with him.

God didn't seem to be restricted by Moses's limited opinion of the matter. He doesn't usually need somebody who's super-duper prepared and super-duper intelligent. He just needs somebody who'll lean on Him, somebody like Moses, who says, "Yes sir, I'll obey, but I can't do it by myself." There he was with all his problems and insecurities—not the least of which was his advanced age—and God helped him to do the impossible.

As long as you stay in the safe zone, you're not going to grow. You can't stay the same and learn at the same time. Many people have been saved, and they're safe from hell. They're on the way to heaven, no question about it. That's fine. But maybe there's more than that. Maybe God is knocking at their door, trying to get their attention, so they'll step out of their safe little houses and step into the baptism of the Holy Spirit and a whole lot more.

Many are so afraid to risk anything that they just stay behind closed doors. It's like they live their entire lives in Egypt, in the land of "not enough." Some people break out and take one step of faith—and they wind up in the wilderness, the land of "just enough." If they continue in a forward direction, living by faith, the day will come when they will enter their promised land. It's the land of milk and honey, a land where the harvest is so great it will boggle your mind. It's a land of more than enough. It's a land where you're walking in the faith zone all the time, so when mountains get in the way, God moves them; and when oceans get in the way, God parts them. It's worth putting in some wilderness time to get there, and it's worth the discomfort of being stretched.

Anytime believers step out of the safety of the old, comfortable way and start to trust God's provision, they have to deal with a huge factor of the unknown. Look how Paul phrased it when he told the elders from the church at Ephesus where he was going next: "Now, behold, I go bound in the spirit unto Jerusalem, *not knowing* the things that shall befall me there" (Acts 20:22, emphasis mine). "Not knowing," he was going anyway. He didn't know whether he would be well received or killed. All he knew was that he was in the will of God. He knew he was bound in the Holy Spirit to make the trip. He didn't know anything beyond that. He was walking into the situation blind. That's living by faith.

Does this apply to something in your life right now? Is there a way that you've held back out of fear of failure or fear of suffering? Have you tried to keep yourself all tucked up in your little safe zone so that you don't have to be vulnerable ever again? Maybe you've been through a divorce and you just don't want to trust anyone ever again. Maybe it's something else. Whatever it is, take a long, hard look at it. Hold it up against some of these scriptures. Remember Paul and Moses and all of the other people who took risks and stepped out of their ruts.

Open yourself up to the Holy Spirit, and tell Him, "Lord, I want to give You my fears. I turn my whole life over to You. I want to live in faith. I believe; help my unbelief! Fill me with courage, and furnish me with faith. I need it. I want to walk in Your will."

Feeding Your Faith

It's all part of the process of dream fulfillment. Every stage of the fulfillment of your dream depends on God. Even the so-called obstacles become important stepping-stones instead of barriers. Let's take a closer look at what I'm talking about. What are some things that you might consider to be obstacles that, in God's view, are merely stages in the process? Here are six that I can think of:

1. Your God-ordained purpose may be threatened, even from its birth.

2. Your God-ordained dream may be contaminated by godless influences.

3. You may experience serious failures.

4. You may be rejected.

5. You may feel personally inadequate.

6. Your God-ordained dream may require an unusually lengthy preparation time.

You can see how any of these could feed discouragement and defeat instead of success. But can you see how they could also feed your faith?

If you get rejected, what's the only way to make that negative event into something positive? The only way is to turn—in faith—to the One who never will reject you. When you do that, you turn the sizable obstacle of rejection into something that is more like a sizable step up toward God. It becomes a sizable step toward the fulfillment of His will for your life.

Think of all of these big-name players in the Bible: Moses, Joseph, David, Paul, Jesus Himself. Think of how often they faced overwhelming obstacles (either of their own making or not—it doesn't matter). Review the Bible accounts about each of them, and hold up their stories against the list above.

Which ones were "survivors," even from birth? Which ones had to prevail against ungodly influences, sometimes for years and years? How many were rejected, misunderstood, put down as a complete failure? How did they handle their long preparation times?

I expect that you can see each of the six so-called obstacles in each of their lives. Now that we know the end of each of their stories, we know who won. We know who succeeded in reaching the goal. We know what kinds of dreams and goals God had in mind for them all along while they were busy working through the details.

Looking at their lives from this perspective puts my life and yours into a whole new light. You can do it. "[Look] unto Jesus, the author and finisher of our faith, who for the joy that was set before Him endured the cross, despising the shame, and has sat down at the right hand of the throne of God" (Heb. 12:2, NKJV).

REVIEW

Living in the Faith Zone

◉ Shamgar killed six hundred Philistines with his oxgoad. He started where he was, used what he had, and did what he could.

◉ In the process of walking toward the fulfillment of your dream, you can expect even the so-called obstacles to become important stepping-stones to faith.

◉ God wants you to live in the "faith zone," and that entails stepping out of your obstacle-free "safe zone."

Chapter 8

DON'T LET GO
OF YOUR DREAM

REACHING YOUR DREAM REQUIRES A process—it takes time, persistence, patience. In this chapter we will discover the importance of holding tightly to your dream and discover how to enjoy the process, even if it takes a long time and leads you through an uncharted course that requires your total faith and commitment.

Ecclesiastes 9:10 says, "Whatever your hand finds to do, do it with your might" (NKJV). That means to give yourself diligently to the task at hand. It involves passion, determination, and excellence. It's the opposite of just getting by or doing the minimum requirement.

The secret to discovering your destiny is to find something you enjoy doing so much that you would be willing to do it for free. Then, become so good at it that people are willing to pay you to do it.

...And Then Some

I want to give you three words that can transform your life: *and then some*. No just surviving and bumping along.

I want to introduce you to an "and then some" person in Genesis 24. It was the custom of the parents to choose whom their children would marry in the Old Testament. As a father of four girls, I'm all for this one!

When it was time for Isaac to be married, his father, Abraham, sent his trusted servant Eleazar to find a wife. Since they didn't have classified ads or computer dating services back then, Eleazar put out a fleece before God, essentially saying, "God, may the right woman you want to marry Isaac offer water for me to drink and my camels also." (See Genesis 24:14.)

He went to the well of water and waited. It was common for women to fetch water for their households, so it stands to reason there were many women going to and from the well. Suddenly a beautiful woman walks up to Eleazar, a complete stranger, and offers him some water. He just watches and observes her quietly as she takes that bucket and dips it in water, and she kindly comes over and says, "Sir, would you like a drink of water?" He probably raised an eyebrow but didn't say a word. "Yes, thank you." And then she says almost matter-of-factly, "Sir, by the way, I will inconvenience myself for a minimum of three to four hours, and I will water your camels also." And Eleazar the servant is just sitting back saying, "Oh, my goodness." Now, we read that, but we don't really understand.

In the Old Testament, it was customary to offer water to a stranger. It was called *the law of hospitality*. It was expected in the New Testament to "be not forgetful to entertain strangers: for thereby some have entertained angels unawares" (Heb. 13:2). It was part of the Hebrew culture that you treat strangers kindly. So, here's the point. When Rebekah walked up to him and said, "Would you like some water?" that was what was required of her. That was what was expected of her. That was normal. But when she added these words, "And I'll water your camels also," everything changed, because what she was saying was, "I'm going to do what is expected of me 'and then some.'"

One of the greatest life lessons that you can ever grab hold of is this: don't just do what's expected. Don't just do what your job description says, what people expect you to do. *Do what's expected and then some.*

The woman had ten camels to water. Camels hold forty gallons of water. Do you understand they had traveled five hundred miles across the desert from Mesopotamia—five hundred miles? The red light on the dashboard was empty, empty, empty, and she had to fill every one of those camels with forty gallons of water. That's four hundred gallons of water total!

> *Don't just do what your job description*
> *says, what people expect you to do.*
> *Do what's expected and then some.*

Here she is. She has runs in her panty hose. She's breaking her fingernails. If that had been most people, they'd have said, "That's not my job. That's not in my job description. I'm only going to do what I'm supposed to do. Here, you take some water, but you take care of your own old, ugly, mangy-looking camels. I'm not going to take care of those camels." But there was something about this woman that grabbed the attention of God Almighty—and she became the great-great-great-great-grandmother of Jesus Christ because of her work ethic. It was because she didn't just give; she gave and then some.

What has happened to the work ethic in America? The philosophy of most people is: "How little can I do and get by with it? I'm just going to do what I'm hired to do. I'm just going to do what's expected of me. I'm just going to do what other people do, and that's enough." But, no, it's not good enough! If you are a Christian, you're supposed to do what you're expected to do—and then some.

The current workplace philosophy in America goes something like this: "I want maximum reward for minimum effort. I want to give the least I can and get back everything I can." With this mentality, what we're raising up is a bunch of shoddy, shabby people who expect something for nothing, and they don't understand the Bible principle of not just doing what you're hired to do or what you're expected to do. Listen to me. The difference between a highly successful person and an average person is those three words—*and then some*. The highly successful person will do what is expected "and then some."

The highly successful athlete will do what is expected, but when the other guys leave the court, he's still out there shooting hoops because he has that "and then some" attitude in him. The highly successful marriage is full of mates who say, "I'm not just going to do what I'm expected to do. It's not fifty-fifty. It's me giving all I'm expected to *and then some*."

Jesus put it like this: "And whoever compels you to go one mile, go with him two" (Matt. 5:41, NKJV). That phrase came from the time period when the Roman soldiers made the Jews carry their armor and their bags. The Jew would be expected to walk a mile. And Jesus would say, "Concerning your enemy and your oppressors, the Roman soldiers, if they ask you to go one mile, because you're a Christian, go two—freely, voluntarily, without them asking you to do it, so you can witness to them of who I am in your life." Jesus said, "Except your righteousness exceed that of the Pharisees, you won't make it into heaven." (See Matthew 5:20.) Well, wait a minute. What was the righteousness of the Pharisees? They were the ultimate clock punchers. They did everything according to the book, and it stopped right there. They would do just exactly what was required and no more. To that, Jesus said, "Your righteousness is not just to be like the Pharisees."

I believe possibly one of the greatest tools for evangelism in this culture is not a pulpit. It could be in the workplace where people don't just do a get-by job. Christians shouldn't go into a job tomorrow morning with the mentality, "I'll do my quota; I'll only do what's expected." But if they went to that workplace every day as a lifestyle, thinking in their mind, "I'm going to do a little bit extra. I'm going to go the second mile. I'm going to do what's expected and go a little bit beyond. And I'm not doing it 'cause the boss is watching. When he's not watching, this is what I do, because my real boss is God, not that boss." If Christians started operating in this principle, do you know what the first question on every job application would be? It would be, "Are you a Christian?" The companies would send recruiters in our church lobby and out in the parking lot and beg us to come to work at their companies, saying, "Please, please, because you're that bunch who doesn't just do what's required and expected, but you're that 'and then some' group."

Everything is blessed because you're
a Christian. That's the witness.

If somebody's paying you money to do something, be thankful, and go to work. Don't be a slacker, because that's your witness. Jesus said, "Let your light so shine before men, that they may see your good works, and glorify your Father which is in heaven" (Matt. 5:16). What? They see how you work, and that gives you a platform into their life. If you want to witness to your boss, give an extra effort every day, and the opportunity will come for you. Then he'll respect your witness. Then he'll come up and say, "Pray for me." But it doesn't happen because you have a bumper sticker and you're handing out tracts. There's nothing wrong with that. I'm not putting that down. But I'm just telling you that there are better ways to be effective.

Mother Teresa was never heckled or interrupted by any group.

Her performance gave her a platform, and she could stand up because they respected her because of how good she was at what she did. We just want a platform without performance. We just think everybody ought to listen to us, but they don't care until they see something in tangible ways that is working for you. They ought to look at your family and see your marriage and your life and your finances. Everything is blessed because you're a Christian. That's the witness.

Rebekah said, "I'm not only going to give you water, sir, but I'm also going to water your camels." Wow! "I'm not only going to fix your car because I'm a mechanic, but I'm also going to wash it, and when you show up, you're going to have the 'wow' factor come on you." "I'm not only going to build you a house, but I'm also going to do this little extra thing just because I'm a nice guy. And I'm not going to charge you. I'm not even going to tell you I did it. I'm going to let you find out on your own." You know what will happen? You know what that builds in people? It builds loyalty. I'll go back to somebody who does something like that for me, even if I have to pay a little bit more. They just got a lifelong customer, because all they did was put three words on the end of their service that I contracted them to do—*and then some.* You'll increase your value tremendously when you do it.

Extra blessings come from extra efforts. We keep praying, "God, prosper us," and God's looking down and saying, "Do something excellent. Do something with the extra effort. Do something beyond what is expected and required." Now, let's apply it to your marriage for just a moment. What would happen if every marriage didn't just do what is required? Divorce courts would dry up. Marriages don't fail because mates are doing extra for each other.

I am responsible for my family. I am responsible for my children. I, as the man, the head of my home, am responsible for the finances. I am responsible. Don't go around shouting that you're the head of the home if you're not willing to take responsibility. And if things aren't right in that home, it is your responsibility. Do what is required and then some. Ed Cole said, "You're male by birth; you're a man by choice." It's not, "How little can I do? This is not on my job description."

Have you heard about the mother of the three preschoolers who was asked if she'd still have children if she had to do it over again? "Sure," she responded. "Just not the same three." You smile, but if your dream is to simply raise your family up in the fear of the Lord, you truly have a great dream and purpose! Don't feel like you have to come up with some other seemingly grand dream before it's important to God.

The assignment of every father and mother is to put their family first and to train them up in the way they should go so that when they are old, they will not depart from it (Prov. 22:6) If you successfully complete that task, you will have accomplished one of life's greatest missions.

We have to teach our children not to grow up with just a "good enough" attitude—just enough to get by…just enough. "The boss isn't here, so let's play. The boss isn't here. Don't do anything. Hey, he doesn't know if you washed this floor or not. Nobody will see if you got that spot over there. It's filthy, but just leave it over there." Well, your real boss is God. And God says, "Do what's required—and then some."

You may say, "Well, I did it, and they didn't notice. They passed me up." But I promise you that if you operate in this principle, God Himself will open up a door and reward you and bless you beyond anything you could ever imagine. "Be faithful in the little things, and I'll make you ruler over many." (See Matthew 25:21.) God said He'd do that. He's called *El Shaddai*, which means the God who is more than enough, not just the get-by God. He's more than enough.

When Rebekah went out there and watered those camels for three to four hours on her own time voluntarily, she had no idea what the ramifications would be. She had no idea that those camels were loaded with diamonds, earrings, rubies, and gold. Read it in Genesis 24. She had no idea. It was just a normal day. She was doing this as a lifestyle. She was a kind person, and she was used to doing what was expected—and then some. How many days had gone by when nobody paid her any attention and rewarded her with nothing? See, that's the deal. She just kept doing what was right in God's eyes.

Eleazar's camels were loaded with gold and precious stones. Talk about incredible wealth! It was hidden in an ugly thing, in a menial thing, in a seemingly insignificant routine thing. It was hidden in going beyond what was required. She didn't know that there was amazing financial reward. She didn't know. See, most of you shoot your camels. Don't shoot your camels. Ride them. She was about to ride that camel that she was watering all the way back to Isaac, her Prince Charming, Mr. Eligible Bachelor, who was born into the wealthiest family on the planet. That old, mangy, ugly situation actually became the gateway to a phenomenal future when she watered it instead of cursing it. I wonder how many times God has sent ugly situations and we just shrugged our shoulders and said, "It's not my problem," and behind that disguise and that ugly situation was an amazing promotion if we'd have just been faithful to do what was required—and then some. From this story,

I see five things you must do to release God's will in your life, five steps to releasing your destiny.

1. Don't despise small things.

Faithfulness with small things brings huge rewards. God is your boss. He's watching you when you're faithful in the small things. Big doors swing on little hinges.

2. Don't wait for the big moments.

Big moments don't come to people who wait for big moments. Big moments come out of faithfulness in little, insignificant moments of doing routine, menial things that are nonglamorous and not really exciting. The big moment comes out of being faithful with the little things. "I wish they'd ask me to sing a solo." Then get in the choir. Come to rehearsal, and let somebody notice you. Have you ever watched a baseball team? A ball game is not made up of great moments. There are only two or three great moments. But a good team just keeps winning.

3. Help people.

Rebekah didn't quote a scripture. She didn't pull out a healing hanky and start spreading oil. No, she just said, "I'm going to help you." Now, isn't that a witness? Isn't that a different approach? Instead of trying to be superspiritual, why don't we just be a nice person and help somebody? She gave a stranger some water and then took care of his camels.

4. Do your best—and then some.

You can't go the second mile until you do the first mile. Can people trust you when they turn their back and walk away and never wonder if you're going to do the job right? If so, you might be a Christian. If you help somebody with their dream, God will reveal yours to you.

5. When God opens the door, walk through it.

Eleazar saw Rebekah, at her own expense and time, serve four hundred gallons of water to those filthy, mangy camels. In Genesis 24:54–56, we see how the story unfolds. Eleazar then, when the task was complete, walked up and said, "Let me tell you who I am, and let me tell you who you are. It just came out of your work ethic. You're the chosen bride-to-be. Come with me." The Bible says that her brother and mother said, "We're excited. We're thrilled about this, but we need ten days." The servant said, "We're not waiting ten days. You come now, or you miss it." Notice that when you give extra effort, it always opens doors. And when God opens the door, don't back up. Don't be intimidated. Don't delay. Don't be embarrassed. Don't say, "I'm not good enough." Don't say, "Well, somebody else could do it better." If God wanted somebody else to do it, He would have put them where you are.

If an opportunity comes your way and God opens a door, stand up, step up, and walk through that door, because God will go with you. God will make up for what you don't have. He will make up for the abilities that you don't have. His anointing will come on you in that situation. How do I know that? It's because I live it in my own life. I've seen Him open doors, and I've thought, "Well, somebody else can do it so much better. Billy Graham should be doing this." No, no! When God opens the door, you walk through it, because apparently He's seen you doing what was required—and then some.

> *When you give extra effort, it always opens doors. And when God opens the door, don't be intimidated.*

See, we keep waiting on supernatural promotion. We say, "Anoint me for promotion." But if you don't do your side on the natural, God can't open the door for the supernatural, because you wouldn't have the integrity and character and work ethic if He does give you that promotion.

"Give Me This Mountain"

When he was in his forties, in the prime of his life, Caleb was one of the twelve spies whom Moses sent out into the Promised Land, which was occupied by other people groups at the time. While he was on that spying mission, Caleb spotted a particular mountain. He wanted it for his own. He figured that he could have dibs on it as the Israelites would come back and conquer the current residents of the land, because he had been the one to spy it out.

This gave Caleb a definite purpose in life, a purpose that was big enough and exciting enough to keep him alive for a long time. He eventually did reach his dream of owning that mountain. But he didn't get to have it quite so fast. In fact, forty long years had to pass before he could even bring it up again. By then, he was eighty-five years old, but God had preserved him, as strong as if he were still in the prime of his manhood so that he would be prepared for that day. Finally, he could say, "Now therefore, give me this mountain of which the LORD spoke in that day" (Josh. 14:12, NKJV).

A lot of delays happened during that forty-year period of time. For starters, right away after Caleb and the other eleven spies had returned, the people of Israel stood in the way. They refused to go to battle to win the land because they were afraid of the giants. No way were they going to risk their lives after the alarming report of most of the spies. Ten of the twelve spies had persuaded Moses and the people to chicken out, which meant that Caleb and Joshua ended up supporting a different vision from the rest of them. Caleb and Joshua got outvoted and overruled.

We know how the story turns out, though. In the end, Caleb got his mountain. His dream became a reality. Let's look at the story of the forty-year process in a little more detail because we can face some of the same hindrances that Caleb did, and we can learn from his experiences.

Fear of giants

Ten of the spies had come back with alarm written all over their faces, saying, "There are giants in the land! We are not able! We are like grasshoppers to those guys! We can't do it! The giants are too big!" The people picked up on their fear. Because of it, the people talked themselves out of a great miracle.

Only Caleb and Joshua had no fear. They had said, "Never mind the giants. Why should we worry about *them*? God wants us to have this land. Look! There are grapes as big as *this*! We are well able to take this land. God will be with us. Let's do it!"

The people just wouldn't buy it. They were like so many of us. Even when we see the evidence of what God is leading us to do, we don't go after it, because we're waiting for the coast to clear. We're waiting until we can take a shot at getting some of the grapes without having to face any giants. We don't understand—there's never any provision without a problem first.

If you're going to hold back and wait until it looks like a problem-free journey ahead, you'll never get the grapes. In fact, you can count on an *increase* in your problems the minute you see a glimpse of God's promised provision. If you intend to reach your promised land, you are just going to have to keep your eyes on those grapes. It's as if those grapes are actually bigger than the giants who grew them.

When David went out to fight the giant Goliath, he did not back down. He knocked Goliath off his feet, and then he cut his head off. To get ahead (pardon the pun), you too are going to have to first face a giant. You are going to have to get close enough to see the whites of his eyes. You are going to have to do it yourself. You cannot send somebody else to do it for you. If you avoid giants because you are afraid, and if you want a giant-free, conflict-free, problem-avoiding life, you will never get ahead at all.

Grasshoppers

Here's what the fearful spies had said: "And there we saw the giants, the sons of Anak, which come of the giants: and we were in our own sight as grasshoppers, and so we were in their sight" (Num. 13:33).

Grasshoppers! That means they perceived themselves as being as little and puny as grasshoppers compared to the inhabitants of Canaan. They thought the giants would be able to just step on them and crush them.

It has always bugged me that they said "grasshoppers." I have always wondered why they didn't at least say, "We seemed like dogs," or some animal a little bigger and stronger than grasshoppers. Grasshoppers can't run or fight. Grasshoppers have wings, but they can't fly. They can only get so high, and then they come back down.

We have wings too, and we're supposed to be able to soar like eagles. Instead, we hop around like grasshoppers. We hop from church to church, from job to job, from marriage to marriage, and from one ministry to another. It seems as though we can't stay put long enough to really face the giants and conquer our mountain.

We don't have to stay that way, though. We can change our self-perception. We can start to soar like eagles if we want to. Our self-perception is so important. How we perceive ourselves is *major*, because other people will pick up on how we perceive ourselves.

Milk and honey?

Another misperception concerns the benefits of where we are going versus what we may have left behind. When the going gets a little tough, sometimes we start to think, as those Israelites did, that we should just go back to where we came from. We forget how bad it was back there. The Israelites said to Moses, "Is it not enough that you have brought us up out of a land flowing with milk and honey to have us die in the wilderness, but you would also lord it over us?" (Num. 16:13, NASU).

"Milk and honey"? What are they talking about? They're all mixed up. The milk and honey is up *ahead*, in the Promised Land, not in Egypt. Reality check! What was life like back in Egypt? The Hebrews ate garlic, leeks, and onions, but milk and honey were never mentioned until now. Back in Egypt, they were *slaves*. All day long, they had to make bricks out of clay and straw. Slaves don't get milk and honey.

Egypt was nowhere near a land of milk and honey for them. It

147

was a land of straw and garlic! But in order to hold them back from reaching what God had in store for them, the enemy had to make them think that where they came from was better. Does this tactic sound a little bit familiar?

Right now, some of us have come out of Egypt by the blood of Jesus. But we find ourselves in the middle of a wilderness. It's hard. We are struggling. We are out of energy, and the fight has gone out of us. We have lost our determination because of all the battles we have been through. All of a sudden, we think, "Hey, wait a minute! I didn't have these problems before I was saved," and that's probably true. Suddenly we want to go back.

I'm telling you, don't leave the border of the land that is truly the land of milk and honey. Let me remind you: what you left behind was death, destruction, and bondage. You left behind the taskmaster and the chains. You don't want to go back to that.

Water from the rock

"Yes," you may object, "but where I am right now sure isn't that great."

I know it's not that great. Part of the problem is that you're not in the promised land yet. Part of the problem is that you have stayed where you are for too long already, and the place that used to be refreshing is all dried up. That's what happened with the children of Israel. Because of hesitation and fear, they ended up staying far too long in what used to be a place of refreshment—and they ran out of water. When that happened, they began to grumble about it.

In desperation, Moses and Aaron sought the Lord, and He told them what to do. (See Numbers 20:2–13.) God wanted them to gather the people together, and then He wanted Moses to take his rod, which represented his authority, and to hold it while he spoke to the rock, which would then produce water. But instead of commanding the rock to produce water, Moses *struck* the rock with his rod.

The rock represents the vision. But instead of speaking to it as God had told him to do, Moses got so aggravated with the demands of the people that he hit it instead.

Antidote to Fear

Below are three fears that you and I face on our journey to the land of dreams.

1. *Fear of faces.* The fear of faces is the fear of people. It's the fear of what people will say, what people will think: "Maybe I'll look stupid. Maybe I'll embarrass myself. I'd better avoid those risks. I'd better stay put and play it safe." No one can make you feel inferior without your consent. Remember, there are two kinds of people who fail: those who listen to nobody and those who listen to everybody! God told them not to be afraid of their faces.

2. *Fear of fences.* This is the fear of barriers and roadblocks. We're afraid that it will be too hard. It might hurt. We might have to work and sweat more than usual. In Moses's case, he could have been thrown into prison or killed for his brazen requests. Nobody had ever done that before—nobody had ever just marched up to Pharaoh and said, "Let my people go!" Charles Lindbergh said, "Success is

not measured by what a man accomplishes but by the opposition he encountered and the courage he maintained in his struggle against it."

3. *Fear of failure.* Isn't that what really stops us every time? We like the idea of success. We like to win. It's the "what ifs" that get us. "What if I fall flat on my face? What if I make a fool of myself? What if...what if..." And the next thing you know, you're back in your easy chair, not going anywhere and not doing anything except holding the remote.

Don't get talked out of your vision.

Moses had presented the vision clearly to the people of Israel. They could stop being slaves, and they wouldn't have to go back to Egypt. God was promising them a land for themselves. All they had to do was obey Him. He would help them. With God on their side, they would prevail over any and all obstacles.

Why was it so hard to do that? What stopped them?

This happens in churches all the time, and it can happen in businesses too. There's a clear goal. The mountaintop is visible up ahead. You're on your way to it. The promise is that you'll get there. Nobody is holding you back.

...except for that person, or usually more than one person, who is sitting right next to you. Or maybe it's you.

Why should the enemy exert himself to muster outside forces to come against you when he will have such an easy time stirring up internal objections? The twelve spies were chosen from the twelve tribes of Israel. They represented a cross section of the people. And they nixed the plan. They ended up being bigger enemies to the plan of God than the giants were. They talked Moses and the other leaders out of trying to acquire the land of promise.

What did God do? He took care of the problem—for a generation at least—by letting them stay "safe," just as they wanted. "Safe" meant they'd have to keep wandering in the wilderness for forty more years while that whole generation died off and a new generation could grow up and replace them.

God's plan could still succeed, only with different players. God would keep their vision alive, but He wouldn't let them fulfill it after all. He would let their sons and daughters fulfill it instead, after the original Exodus people died off.

REVIEW

Don't Let Go of Your Dream

⊙ The secret to discovering your destiny is to find something you enjoy doing so much that you would be willing to do it for free.

⊙ Don't just do what your job description says. Do what's expected *and then some.*

⊙ If an opportunity comes your way and God opens a door, stand up, step up, and walk through that door, because God will go with you.

⊙ Don't get talked out of your vision.

Chapter 9

KEEP CLIMBING

ADMIRAL JOE FOWLER WAS IN THE United States Navy during both World War I and World War II. He was a naval architect, and during World War II, he was in charge of West Coast ship construction. Among his many notable accomplishments, he was the designer of the two largest aircraft carriers of the time, the USS *Lexington* and the USS *Saratoga*. Mission accomplished. He retired after the war from the navy in 1948 at the age of fifty-four.

A short time later, Walt Disney looked him up. Disney had a dream of building an extravagant family theme park in California. He figured that if Fowler could successfully handle everything he had done in the military, he would have the know-how to head up the design and construction of the park, which he wanted to call Disneyland. Fowler felt he was up to the challenge, and he accepted the job. Not only did Fowler head up the design and construction process, but he also managed the park's operations for years after Disneyland opened in 1955.

A decade later, Disney had a new dream—to build a similar theme park on the other side of the United States, in Florida. He wanted to call it Walt Disney World, and he persuaded his friend Joe Fowler to be in charge of designing and constructing that one too. The Florida project came with even more challenges, not the least of which was creating the park in the midst of thousands of acres of swampland. By now, Fowler was seventy-one, and most people his age were taking it easy. But he said yes again. By the time it was finished in 1971, he was seventy-seven.[1] Now he could retire.

But when he was eighty-seven years old, his friend Disney asked him to help with the design of the new Epcot park next to Walt Disney World. At eighty-seven? They had to persuade him harder this time. They flew him down to the site, and they showed him this new mission. Nobody had ever seen such a thing before, and they wanted him to build it. The fire lit up in his eyes. He said yes again.

Around that time, somebody interviewed him and asked,

"Why in the world at eighty-seven would you take such a huge project on?"

Fowler's reply? "You don't have to die until you want to." He completed the Epcot project with time to spare, finally laying down his drafting board at the age of ninety-nine in 1993. As far as Joe Fowler was concerned, as long as he had a purpose and a mission, he had no limits. He was famous for saying, in response to Disney's most outrageous demands, "Can do!"[2]

Breaking Limitation Thinking

Clearly, Admiral Joe Fowler was not afflicted with what I call "limitation thinking." He was confident, humble, and motivated, all at the same time, and as a result, he accomplished a legendary amount in his lifetime, more than several ordinary people.

To accomplish even lesser goals, most of us, however, seem to have to break through quite a few limitations in our thinking, especially if we are going to succeed on God's terms for God's purposes. Our limitations are mostly in our minds, often in our spirits, and sometimes in our bodies. To fulfill the vision God gives us for our lives, we have to break through old ways of thinking and acting. How we turn out spiritually and physically has so much to do with our minds.

Mountains Are for Climbing

In the Swiss Alps, there is a little mountain day camp for rookie climbers. Many businesses go there and take their employees for an outing. What they'll do is this: they'll start out early in the morning and load on their climbing gear, and then they'll climb halfway up a mountain. When they get halfway up, there's something they call "the halfway house." They get there around noon. They take off their gear, go in for a warm meal, and sit in front of the beautiful fireplace. It's a beautiful environment.

To fulfill the vision God gives us for our lives, we have to break through old ways of thinking and acting.

The trip sponsors say that every time, without exception, when it's time for lunch to be over and time to strap their gear back on, they lose half the people. Half of them are content to stay and never complete the journey. They're content to go only halfway up.

So, they stay in the halfway house and lounge around and play games and sing by the piano. They sit by the fire and enjoy themselves. Then around four o'clock in the afternoon, they all hear a bell outside. They walk over and look out the big window that faces the mountain. That's when they see their friends summiting that mountain! The halfway house hosts say the party atmosphere turns instantly into a funeral atmosphere, because now the people who chose to stay behind realize that their friends, who were willing to keep going, have just had the experience of a lifetime, while they stayed behind, complacent and settled. Now they wish they could be celebrating on the mountaintop too, but it's too late.

This is a picture of how our lives can be, isn't it? Many times, it would seem to be easier just to settle. Why bother continuing to hold out hope that you will possess your mountain, let alone hope that you will ever climb it? Why not just be a quitter? Why not go back down to the valley, where life is easier? It's hard work to be a mountain climber. It's much easier to wimp out. But, of course, it's obvious that you'll never reach your mountaintop if you quit.

Quitters

We all know some quitters. Quitters just don't try anymore. They tend to be "victims" of something or somebody, and they can become bitter and depressed. It's kind of a drag to be around them. Quitters wish things would be easier. They don't have a lot of endurance. They want to opt out of all the tests and trials and training.

When things get the least bit difficult, quitters quit. When adversity rears its head, they opt out. Quitters are the people who jump out of their marriages. They abandon their careers. They're the ones who quit believing in God when unexplainable trouble occurs.

Just to forewarn you, there are two times when you'll be the most vulnerable to quitting. The first is when you've suffered a great failure. The second, believe it or not, is when you've just had a great success. The first one isn't a surprise. And the second one isn't either, if you think about it, because after you succeed, you can soon become complacent. It happens to whole organizations sometimes. They reach for high goals and achieve them, and then they just rest on their laurels. They aren't hungry anymore. They lose their edge. They forget about how they got there. They even forget about God.

Paul was not a quitter. He never quit. Even when he was in prison, he was still climbing his mountain. He didn't minimize the hardships, but he pressed past them. He said, "We are afflicted in every way, but not crushed; perplexed, but not despairing; persecuted, but not forsaken; struck down, but not destroyed; always carrying about in the body the dying of Jesus, so that the life of Jesus also may be manifested in our body" (2 Cor. 4:8–10, NASU).

The life of Jesus included a lot of suffering. That never stopped Him. Look what He did, especially when He went ahead and climbed Calvary. He was definitely not a quitter. We're supposed to imitate Him: "[Look] unto Jesus the author and finisher of our faith; who for the joy that was set before him endured the cross, despising the shame, and is set down at the right hand of the throne of God" (Heb. 12:2).

Campers

You can see where I'm headed with this. We're talking about mountain climbing and breaking through limitation thinking, and we've just covered the quitters, the ones who hardly get started.

There are two times when you'll be the most vulnerable to quitting: when you've suffered a great failure and when you've just had a great success.

Then we come to the campers, the ones who climb for a while and then decide they like it well enough halfway up the mountain. They decide to camp out and enjoy the view. They let the real climbers keep going, and they don't seem to remember that they were once climbers themselves.

Campers go so far, but not all the way. They achieve some aspect of their goal, and then they're satisfied. Their attitude is, "Well, this is pretty good. It's better than most people. It's comfortable right here. I think I'll pitch my tent and stay awhile."

They grow weary of the never-ending climb.

Campers join the halfway club. They're not total quitters, but they're not going to make it to the top any more than the quitters are. They prefer to hang around with other campers and roast marshmallows over the fire. They reminisce about their adventures when they were climbers.

The other campers won't challenge them. They like each other's company, and they don't want to motivate each other to break camp. As a group, they've lost their edge. They begin to see the campground as their permanent address. They have achieved partial success, and that seems to be enough for them. They are an example of the saying: "*Good* is the enemy of *best*."

Climbers

God wants you to be a climber. Just as He showed Caleb his mountain and kept him working toward it, He gives you a dream, and He wants to help you reach it.

To be a climber, you have to be dedicated. You have to put up with discomfort and fatigue. You may get to a level place where you could pitch a tent and camp out, but you will resist the temptation. Climbers adopt the mentality that camping places are like base camps. In their view, what they have achieved up to that point is the launching pad for the future, not their final address. They see their hammocks as springboards more than as places to relax.

The mountain you are climbing may look insurmountable. Now that you're climbing it, you may not be able to see the top of it anymore. You may be climbing a mountain of debt, or of marital problems, or of sickness. About now, it would be so easy to be a quitter or a camper.

But if you are a climber, you just keep putting one foot in front of the other. You take your provisions and refreshment where you can get them, while keeping your ultimate goal in the front of your mind. "I am climbing this mountain because I'm going to conquer it. I am going to reach the top."

Climbers are the people who see obstacles as opportunities. They see the glass as half-full when others see it half-empty. Climbers are the people who know that a bend in the road is not the end of the road. They're the people who, regardless of misfortune and disadvantage, pain or past achievements, keep on climbing until they reach the top. They may get bruised and sore, but they get over it. To make a lame analogy, climbers are like the *Mona Lisa*—she keeps smiling, even when her back's against the wall.

Eventually, you will make it. But did you know that the most dangerous time for a climber isn't while the climber is still going up? The most dangerous time is coming back down. That says to me that you need to keep your climbing mentality even after you've achieved your desire. You need that same level of concentration and determination. You need to stay focused. You need to keep yourself from getting complacent just because you've accomplished the thing you set out to do. After your climb succeeds, it's still not time to camp out or to quit.

If you're a climber, you will hear things from God whether you're headed up or whether you're headed back down. He will be climbing with you. Jesus climbed mountains, literally. And often

He had His disciples and followers climb with Him. Because they climbed with Him, He taught them things. (See Matthew 5:1–2.)

The disciples and the people who climbed with Jesus learned things that the people back down in the valley did not get to learn. The Son of God shared things with them because they were His climbing companions.

There's a difference between growing old in the Lord and growing up in Him.

They didn't quit, and they hadn't become complacent back at the first rest stop. They not only made physical progress by climbing, but they were climbing mental and spiritual mountains too. If we're going to be like them, we have to get *up* and keep going. We have to go *up out* of our valley of Egypt and keep climbing until we reach the top of our mountain.

We have to grow up in the Lord. There's a difference between growing old in the Lord and growing up in Him. Lots of people say, "Well, I go to church." Well, I'm sure God's impressed, but your life may not be much of a mountain-climbing expedition. You may be just putting in time instead of taking ground from one victory to another, "from glory to glory" (2 Cor. 3:18).

You are not old until your regrets take the place of your dream. That never happened to Caleb. He never looked back with regret. Neither did Paul. His mission in life was a whole different kind of mountain from Caleb's, and here is his attitude toward it: "One thing I do, forgetting those things which are behind and reaching forward to those things which are ahead, I press toward the goal

161

for the prize of the upward call of God in Christ Jesus" (Phil. 3:13–14, NKJV).

Regret looks back. Worry looks around. Vision looks up. Vision sees the mountaintop even when the clouds hide it from view. Enduring the climb now equals enjoyment later. Breaking through limitations and barriers now equals victory later.

God will help you climb. He will climb with you, and He will lend you a hand every day. He will help you break through limitation thinking, and He will help you climb your mountain. Ultimately, as Sir Edmund Hillary said after conquering Mount Everest, "It is not the mountain we conquer but ourselves."

REVIEW

Keep Climbing

- God does not have any limits. But we do—or we *think* we do. He will help us break through limitation thinking. All things are possible with Him!

- You need to press forward, keeping your dream alive, not only breaking through fears, misconceptions, lies from the enemy, and bad advice, but also learning to ignore the voice that tells you to take it easy.

- God wants you to be a *climber*, not a quitter or a camper.

⊚ Regret looks back. Worry looks around. Vision looks up. Vision sees the mountaintop even when the clouds hide it from view. Breaking through limitations and barriers now equals victory later.

Chapter 10

NEVER DOUBT
YOUR VISION

WHAT DO YOU DO WHEN YOUR world does not look like your word; when you have a word from God over your life, but your present situation doesn't look like the dream God gave you?

God told Abraham, "You have security. You have success. You have servants. You have wealth. You have everything. But I want you to walk away from it." Hebrews 11:8 put it like this: "By faith Abraham, when called to go to a place he would later receive as his inheritance, obeyed and went, even though he did not know where he was going" (NIV). He knew where he was, but he didn't know where he was going.

In Genesis 22, the opposite was true for Abraham. Now he knows where he's going, but he doesn't know where he is. The man of faith is confused! The dilemma has broken his compass, and he doesn't know where he is. He doesn't understand a thing that God is doing. What's going through his mind is, "God, where are You? I'm lost. I'm confused. All I know is that I heard a voice, and the voice said, 'Go.' But I don't know where I am right now. I know You made me a promise, but where I am doesn't look like anything You showed me in my spirit." He was three days from "a place." It's a place I'm going to call "three days from nowhere."

"After These Things . . . "

Chapter 22 starts out by saying, "After these things . . . " After what things? I believe Abraham thought the worst trials of his faith were in his past. I believe he thought he had finally arrived, because now he had Isaac, his promised seed. He had the promise.

The trials of his past included the trauma of leaving Ur of the Chaldeans and everything that he had. Then it was telling his wife, "Sarah, get everybody together. Load the wagon. We're going."

"Where are we going?"

"I don't know. God just said we're going, and He'll let me know when we get there." That's a trauma! That's a faith walk. No doubt behind his back, people were saying, "He's crazy! He's gone off the deep end."

It didn't end there. Next came the trauma of splitting with Lot, his own family. The trauma of Sodom and Gomorrah followed. On the heels of that, he saw his other son, Ishmael, disappear into a desert, and he was left with questions as to why he would never see his boy again.

If that wasn't enough, then his wife Sarah was kidnapped and placed in the harem of a wicked king who was going to rape her if he had his way. What a trauma. What a testing. What a trial. How he had to trust God. How he had to believe God through every stage that he went through.

This is the trial of a lifetime, and if you'll hold on, it's going to become the blessing of a lifetime.

Sometimes you think your big trials are in your past. If God's going to introduce greater revelations of who He is and greater dimensions of His power, it will be "after these things."

Just when you think you've been through it all, seen it all, and fought every demon that hell could bring, here comes the big one—the trial of a lifetime!

"After these things," God said to Abraham, "leave where you are and go a three days' journey, and I'll tell you what to do."

He takes his boy, Isaac, to that mountain. *Isaac* means "laughter" in Hebrew because his mother laughed at the very idea of conceiving him. She was ninety-nine years old when God said, "You're going to get pregnant," and she laughed. God let her know that the last laugh would be on her. "I will give you Isaac, and you're going to name him 'laughter.'"

God's biggest point to Abraham was this: "Though you're one hundred twenty years old, don't relax! I know you think your big trials are in the past, but I'm not through with you. And the way that you know I'm not through with you is that I'm going to do something mighty in your future. You'll know it because I have to send you through a season of trials, of feeling like you're confused and lost...a time when you will be 'three days from nowhere.'"

Three Days From Nowhere

"Abraham, you may not know where I am, and you may not know what's going on. That's a sign that I'm about to trust you with your greatest blessing yet! So take your last laugh. Take Isaac, 'laughter,' put him on an altar, and kill him!"

Sometimes when you're "three days from nowhere," you are in a mind battle. You're confused. You don't know where God is. You don't know where you are. You know where you're going, but this doesn't look like where you're supposed to be at this time in your life. At this phase, you thought you would be further along. Instead, you're "three days from nowhere"!

Everybody has his or her trial of a lifetime. The other trials are just faith boosters to get your immune system up. Then comes the big one, the trial of a lifetime.

Sometimes when you're "three days from nowhere," you are in a mind battle.

But it's the trial of a lifetime that leads to the experience of a lifetime. The Bible says three times that Abraham lifted up his eyes. In Genesis 18:2 he lifted up his eyes and saw three men at his tent door. One of them was God, and he fed Him a meal. At that point, God started giving promises. He said, "As the sand…upon the sea shore," so shall your seed be (Gen. 22:17).

So, the first level, when he lifted up his eyes, is the receiving of the promise.

But then the scripture says again in Genesis 22:4, "Abraham lifted up his eyes, and saw the place afar off." Now it's gone beyond just receiving the promise. You actually begin to step into the destiny that God has for you. There's one other level that you get to, though, and that's in Genesis 22:13: "Abraham lifted up his eyes…and behold behind him a ram…"

You only get that level of blessing when you go through "three days from nowhere." When you go through such a severe trial of a lifetime, it feels like everything is gone, you were lost, you have missed God, you somehow have messed up, the enemy eats you up with self-condemnation, and you feel like you've blown it and messed up.

The truth is, God has to bring all men and women whom He has a destiny for to a place called "three days from nowhere." It's the place where you're saying, "I know where I'm going, but I sure don't understand where I am right now. I don't have a clue what's going on. This is not what You showed me, Lord."

The Scripture says that God proved and showed Himself to be Jehovah-Jireh at that place (Gen. 22:14). Abraham did not call Him Jehovah-Jireh when he got to the mountain and saw the provision. He called Him Jehovah-Jireh down at the foot of the mountain when his boy asked him, "Father, where's the lamb?" Abraham said, "God will provide himself a lamb" (Gen. 22:7–8).

Anybody can call Him Jehovah-Jireh when you get on top of the problem, but when you're "three days from nowhere" and you don't know where to turn, you don't know what to do, you don't know why you've had this X-ray come back, and your husband left you for another woman...that's when you're "three days from nowhere."

When you don't know why you paid your tithes, but now you're laid off, it makes no sense. You're three days from nowhere. You didn't think you'd be here at this stage. At this point in your life, you never dreamed that you would be a widow, here by yourself in your senior years. But the Lord sent me to tell you that you don't wait until you get on the mountain to call Him Jehovah-Jireh. Abraham called Him Jehovah-Jireh when he was still three days from nowhere!

If you're three days from nowhere, God's letting you know that He's with you. You may not know where you're going, but you know who's going with you. And if He's with you, it doesn't matter what you're going through!

Don't wait until you get on the mountain to call Him Jehovah-Jireh.

I was with a couple in our church when their four-year-old son died in their arms. I'll never forget them holding the lifeless body of that four-year-old boy, weeping, crying. They were three days from nowhere.

It's only a matter of time before you're faced with such a severe trial that you find yourself "three days from nowhere." You have no answers, no clichés, no one-liners that somebody can zing at you and bring you out of it! You're confused, you're stunned, and you feel a little hurt by God.

Let me give you a little pastoral advice. The biggest room in your brain had better be reserved for things you don't understand. If you have to understand everything before you will trust and serve God, you don't understand the concept of faith!

God doesn't always give us explanations. He did say, "In the mount of the LORD it shall be seen" (Gen. 22:14). Did you catch that? "It shall be seen." There's a place God takes you where you see things through the Lamb's eyes.

I heard someone say that when you're in the will of God, everything will be good, and there'll never be any storms. What a joke! Jesus told the disciples to go to the other side of the river. They got in the boat, moved on what He told them to do, and were in the perfect will of God. Then comes up the biggest storm you've ever seen.

Be careful how you talk about people. Don't presume they missed God or that they're not in touch with His will. They might be in the will of God and be in a big storm. They could be in the perfect storm with all hell raging around them. But listen, if you get in a storm in the will of God, lift up your eyes. It won't be long before somebody will come walking on the water to see about you!

Can you see Abraham as he raised the knife? God said, "Now I know. Now I know. Stop, Abraham. Now I know. I had to put you through the trial of a lifetime to reveal to you the greatest revelation of who 'the Lamb' is."

You cannot get from this place to the place that God's trying to take you to without walking through seasons of not understanding. You may ask yourself, "Where am I? Why is this happening? Where is God when I hurt? What's going on? Why do bad things always happen to good people?"

I've been three days from nowhere many times in my ministry. Just when I thought I had seen it all, God would shift me to a place called "three days from nowhere."

I remember an occasion that stands way out to me. We had just gotten into what was at that time the new sanctuary, and what a tremendous pressure there was on my wife and me. We were so young when we took over Free Chapel. She was eighteen when I married her, and I tried so hard to make her into what I thought a preacher's wife should be. I didn't know that God had a special design for her and she could be who she was. She didn't have to be what I thought was a preacher's wife.

My efforts to change her caused tremendous problems in our marriage during those early years. I was trying to make her sit up front in church. I was trying to make her do things that she did not want to do. Because of that, we began to develop issues in our relationship. Soon after that, our first two daughters were born.

I can remember one Saturday in particular. It seemed like we just had a meltdown in our marriage. That night we basically said to each other these words: "I still love you, but I'm not in love with you anymore." We both had built up things in our hearts. I finally said, "I'm a hypocrite. I can't go preach anymore. I can't go to that pulpit anymore."

We called my in-laws and asked them to come to the house to help us through it.

I called the associate pastor to ask him to preach Sunday, but I didn't tell him why because, you know, when you're in the ministry, you can't do what I'm doing right now. You can't tell anybody you're not superhuman! You can't tell anybody that you hurt.

I'll never forget that day when Pat, my mother-in-law, came. We were in the bedroom upstairs. Cherise said, "I'm coming home, Mama. I'm coming home."

Pat said, "You're not coming to my house! You said 'for better or for worse.' This is your home. This is your marriage. Those children are going to have a daddy and a mama, and you two are going to make it work now even if we have to stay here and fast and pray till we're a bunch of skeletons. We're going to make it work!"

We were three days from nowhere! I'm glad we didn't quit. I'm glad we didn't walk away. We were confused, hurting, and broken, but we got through it. We got it fixed.

Some years later, "after these things," there came a trial of a lifetime as trouble broke out in the church. As an inexperienced young pastor, I made huge mistakes. My heart was for God, but sometimes I'm just human, and I make bad decisions!

I began to receive anonymous letters. I hate anonymous letters to this day. But during that particular season, I would get them daily, saying, "You've lost it." "God has withdrawn His anointing." "God is through with you." "The ministry is going to fail." "God has withdrawn His Holy Spirit from that place."

It went on for almost a year. I watched our biggest tither walk away as demons whispered in my ear, "I told you. I told you that you were a failure." All the while, I didn't know that, while I was climbing that mountain, other tithers were coming up the other side of the mountain by the hundreds. But you don't know this when you're three days from nowhere!

I remember one particular day vividly. I'll never forget it as long as I live. I was just having one of those days. I put my hands on my face in the office on my desk, and I just broke and began to weep. My secretary at the time was Susan Page. She's been like a second mother to Cherise and me. She walked in and said, "Oh, Pastor." That's all she said. And then she began to pray in the Holy Ghost, and she laid her hands on me praying, "Oh, Pastor."

I was three days from nowhere. This ministry was three days from nowhere. Every demon in hell said, "Leave. Give up. Quit. God's through with you." Reading this book, somebody is three days from nowhere in your marriage or three days from nowhere in the dream that God's given you—and it seems as though God's brought you into a place of confusion. You don't understand a thing that's going on, and you've cried out.

It's almost like while I was writing this book, I heard in prayer the author in the Book of Revelation saying, "There were voices that were crying out from beneath the altar, 'How long, O Lord? How long?'" I heard those voices in my spirit. As I was praying, I heard people crying, "How long, O Lord?" I've just come to tell you that you're not out of the will of God. You're three days from nowhere. This is the trial of a lifetime, and if you'll hold on, it's going to become the blessing of a lifetime. You will see the Lamb in all of His glory.

Maybe you're someone who's going through divorce. Perhaps you're going through a dark season—you don't understand why your world doesn't look like the one God gave you. You're three days from nowhere.

You know what Abraham called his trial of a lifetime? He said, "I go to the mountain to worship." He took the most severe trial of his life and turned it into worship.

Every true dream God gives will make the same trek as Abraham's dream made through the place of confusion. You'll wake up one day and find yourself three days from nowhere. But remember, on Friday they crucified our Lord. Three days later, He rose again. You may feel confused, broken, and discouraged. You're just three days from nowhere. It's Friday, but Sunday's coming!

Even though your promise may be postdated, remember whose signature is on the check!

Wait! Your appointment is still on God's calendar. "There has never been the slightest doubt in my mind that the God who started the great work in you would keep at it and bring it to a flourishing finish" (Phil. 1:6, THE MESSAGE).

God works on both ends of the timeline. He gets you ready for "it" (even when you don't know what "it" is) and He gets "it" ready for you. Even though your promise may be postdated, remember whose signature is on the check! To get from where you are to where you're going, you have to be willing to be in between. Have you been asking the Lord how long your passion and dream will be "there" while your place is "here"? Have you been wondering how long the Lord will show you where you are going yet leave you in confusion where you are? Remember: just before He opens new doors and new opportunities that give birth to new dreams, you'll go through a place called "three days from nowhere." When you do, never doubt your vision.

Never Doubt Your Vision

The reason I called this chapter "Never Doubt Your Vision" is because I know that God will back up the dreams and visions that He puts into people's hearts. You should never doubt your vision because you should never doubt your God.

It doesn't matter how long it takes to see your dream come to fruition. It doesn't matter if your vision is a big one or a little one. If God is in it, it's in the bag. If He inspired it in the first place, He will see it through to completion.

So what if they don't believe?

So what if "they" say it won't happen? So what if people laugh and mock the dream that God has given you? They mocked Noah when he started building an ark in the middle of a drought, but he's the one who had the last laugh.

The simple fact is this: Your God is a rock. He will not fail. He won't even miss a step.

Other people don't have to believe in you in order for your dream to come true. It's your dream. God gave it to *you*, not to them. They don't have to believe. It's not up to them at all. They're not the ones who are carrying that dream on the inside of them as you are. You're the dream carrier, and what God plans to do does not depend upon the affirmation of the people around you. Paul said, "For what if some did not believe? shall their unbelief make the faith of God without effect? God forbid: yea, let God be true, but every man a liar; as it is written" (Rom. 3:3–4).

Paul knew what he was talking about, because when he got knocked off his horse on the road to Damascus, the church people found it very hard to believe that Paul (Saul of Tarsus, who had persecuted the church mercilessly) had even become a Christian, let alone to trust that God had a plan for using him. Naturally, they thought he was faking it. (See Acts 9:26.)

But it didn't matter to Paul. Paul just kept hanging on to his vision and to the Lord, who had given it to him. He faced all the opposition calmly. He probably expected it. He models for us what I call "stand-alone" faith, the kind of faith that keeps moving forward, even in the face of disbelief and antagonism.

When all the voices around you tell you that you cannot accomplish the dream that God has given you and that it will not happen, God wants to give you that kind of faith. He wants you to be able to say, "So what if they don't believe? They can't cancel out what God has put into me."

When you have a real dream, "they" can throw you into a pit and your dream will still happen! Remember Joseph? When you have a real dream, "they" can lie about you and defame your good name. They can accuse you of crimes you didn't commit. That's what happened when Potiphar's wife accused Joseph of raping her. But even if they throw you into prison, your dream isn't locked up. Even if "they" overlook you for promotion and ignore you and act as if they never heard of you, God will see your dream through. So what if they don't believe?

If you have a real dream from God, it won't die in the face of opposition. So what if nobody has ever done your dream before?

So what if even talented and qualified people have tried and failed to do what you believe God has anointed you to do? So what if the doctor has never seen anybody recover from what you have? So what? Let God be true and every man a liar!

How can you be sure?

Everything I said above applies to you only if your dream matches God's plan for your life. How can you be sure it does?

If it's not God's dream, He's not obligated to back it up. *You need to identify the origin of your dream.* Not all dreams are God's dreams.

Many times, people say they have a dream, but it's really somebody else's dream. Sometimes parents are bad in this regard. They want to relive some part of their life through you, so they assign something to you that *they* always wanted to do. They didn't get to do it, so they want their child to do it. That sets you up for a lifetime of trying to please your mother or father. You try to please and appease and get their approval even after you become an adult. Finally one day, you wake up and realize that you are trying to live up to somebody else's dream. You're trying to fulfill somebody else's expectations. It may not even have been God's plan for your momma or your daddy, and here you are stuck with it.

> *You need to identify the origin of your dream. Not all dreams are God's dreams.*

It doesn't matter how many years you have spent trying to chase that dream—if it's not *your* dream from God, don't bother with it. Don't let anyone cram a dream into your heart that just doesn't fit.

Another kind of dream that you should stop carrying is the kind that's tainted by pride or jealousy or anger or rejection. Are you trying to prove something to somebody? Don't go there. Are you trying to do something that will finally show your daddy that you're as good as your sister? Are you trying to garner praises? Are you trying to prove things to your brother or your cousin or your ex?

Are you trying to make up for being rejected? Ask the Lord to help you get past it. Ask Him to give you a real dream straight from heaven, a dream that He can back up.

Take inventory.

You also have to *determine the resource of your dream*. You have to take inventory of the gifts and talents and resources that God has given you and see if they match up with the dream you think is from God.

Do it honestly. Don't say you have talents you *wish* you had. Don't lie to yourself.

Your resources, gifts, and talents should provide an indication of what God's dream is for your life. They should also let you know some things that you're *not* gifted to do so that you don't go out and try to do them (and fail).

I believe that when God gives you a dream, He supplies you with everything you need to fulfill that dream. What He gives you may be only the raw material, and you may be responsible for turning it into more—like when you take that good mind of yours and educate it through years of schooling—but He will have given you the basics.

You won't have to beg, borrow, or steal someone else's resources in order to fulfill your dream from God. You can just relax and trust God to collect your own resources at the right time and in the right way. You won't have to do something as Sarah did when she couldn't fulfill her God-given dream to have a child. She jumped the gun. She sent her husband to sleep with her servant girl, Hagar, because she couldn't imagine how God was going to get her pregnant at her age in life. She was too quick to evaluate her own resources with her own limited experience.

You don't have to wish you were somebody else. In fact, you insult your Creator when you do that. He made you the way He wanted to. Don't try to masquerade as somebody else. God says, "I'm not going to use somebody else for this one. You're going to push this one out!"

He made you for a purpose, and He wants you to walk in it.

Let Him mold you the way a potter molds clay. Don't tell Him He messed up. Don't insult Him by shopping around for another set of gifts. Just inventory your resources and spend time with God talking about them. He may have given you some hidden ones that you don't know about. Let Him be your Lord.

REVIEW

Never Doubt Your Vision

- Never doubt your vision. If God gave it to you, even if it seems far away, you can count on His help to achieve it.

- Let God adjust your vision if He needs to. He usually needs to make some changes inside you before you're ready to pursue your dream.

- Be looking for your next mountain. God wants to give you another vision that will build on this one.

- Don't be discouraged if other people don't agree with your vision. They don't have to for it to be valid. Decide if your dream is really from God, and then go for it with your whole heart.

Chapter 11

NEVER TOO OLD

JUST WHEN YOU THINK YOU CAN RETIRE, JUST when you start to think, "I'm sixty-five, and I'm sliding for home," don't be surprised if God puts a new mantle on you. You see, God has a plan for your life in the *now*. Just when you think you have your golden years all sewn up and you've told the people at the golf course that they are going to start seeing your smiling face a lot, don't be too shocked if a new kingdom career comes knocking.

Whether you're old or not, married or not, settled and secure or not, you need to know that your God has a purpose and a mission for you right now. How can I be so sure that He does, when I don't even know you? Because you're still here. That means God has preserved you for *something*.

Just when you think you have your golden years all sewn up, don't be too shocked if a new kingdom career comes knocking.

Jacob was an old man when his son Joseph was taken to Egypt. His boy Joseph had been his dream. Now Jacob thought his dream was dead. But in Genesis 45, we see that his spirit was revived. Joseph was still alive! The old man got his dream back in his old age.

As long as you have a purpose, you'll keep on living. You're never too old for God. Moses was eighty years old when God gave him his assignment. Caleb was eighty-five when God gave him his mountain.

You can say to yourself, "The rest of my years will be the best years of my life." David said, "Teach us to number our days" (Ps. 90:12). He could have said, "Teach us to add years to our lives and life to our years." The path of the righteous grows brighter and brighter, not darker and darker. "The path of the righteous is like the light of dawn, that shines brighter and brighter until the full day" (Prov. 4:18, NASU).

Father Abraham

If anybody could have retired comfortably, it would have been Abraham. He was a wealthy man. He was seventy-five years old. He had settled in a lush valley, and he had vast herds of cattle and sheep. According to some commentaries, he had at least one thousand servants. But then God came knocking. Genesis 12:1–4 tells how God told him to pack up and leave his land and his countrymen behind and to launch on a journey—to somewhere. God didn't say where. He did promise to make a great nation of his offspring. But wait a minute—Abraham and Sarah had never had any children, and now they were too old.

I'm sure his wife wondered if he was in his right mind. "Honey, what do you mean we're leaving here? You've worked all your life to make this place what it is. This place represents your life's work. You're seventy-five years old. I'm sixty-five. What do you mean we're going to start living in tents? Where are we going? What do you mean you 'don't know'?"

Abraham (who was still called "Abram" at the time) just said, "I realize I don't know where we're going. I only know God has called me. He'll make a way for us. We have to go because we have to obey God."

Father Abraham—who wasn't actually a father because he had no children yet, and sometimes I think that could be why he took his nephew Lot along with him when he left—had no concept of the importance of his decision. What was God's mission for Abraham? It was no less than to populate the entire Middle

East! The mission and purpose that he said yes to involved the establishment of the Jews, God's own people, in their own land. Abraham would become the father of so many generations that nobody would be able to count them. "More than the grains of sand on the sea shore," was how God put it later. (See Genesis 22:17–18.)

What made him do it?

Why would an old guy like Abraham pack up and leave for the wilderness? What made him do it? I see four or five dynamics at work, and you can learn a few things from them—even if you're not anywhere near the age of seventy-five yet.

Here is what I observe about Abraham. He had the following in his life:

- The ability to hear God

- The ability to believe what God said

- The ability to denounce security for the sake of God's mission

- The ability to stay focused on the mission

- The ability to accomplish the mission

We've talked about some of these things in earlier parts of this book, but not from this perspective. Let's see what we can learn.

He had the ability to hear God.

We read, "The Lord had said unto Abram..." *How* did the Lord say it? Was it an audible voice? Maybe. It couldn't have been a "word" from the Word the way we talk about it today, because, obviously, there were no Bibles yet. There were no pulpits. There didn't seem to be any prophets roaming the countryside that God could have given a word to.

All we know is that Abram had the ability to hear what God said. That implies that he had some kind of a relationship with the Lord. He recognized the voice of the Lord because he had heard it before.

How does that apply to you and me? How do we hear the voice? Even with our Bibles and other people around us who can help us hear God, the same basic, underlying relationship with God is a prerequisite. You will never really hear God until you have developed a relationship with Him. Then you'll recognize His voice. When He speaks, even if it's without words, it will sound like thunder in your spirit. When God speaks, you just *know* it's Him.

If you say, "Well, that's never happened to me," then you should be asking for a closer relationship with Him. Christianity is not religion. It's not about candles and statues and rituals and buildings and programs. It's about relationship, walking with the Lord, like the line from the old hymn, "He walks with me, and He talks with me, and He tells me I am His own."[1]

When He speaks, even if it's without words, it will sound like thunder in your spirit.

If you will spend time in the Word and start reading it every day, and if you start praying and talking to Him, your ability to hear God will increase dramatically. It's the same with the people you love. The more you spend time with them, the better you understand them. Spend time with God. Become His friend, and you will recognize His voice when He speaks to you.

You need to press into your relationship with Him. Paul said that it's "not as though I had already attained, either were already perfect: but I follow after, if that I may apprehend that for which also I am apprehended of Christ Jesus" (Phil. 3:12). Paul kept trying to "apprehend" the Lord, having been captured by His love.

In other words, God doesn't save you and show you His power just to get you to heaven. He wants you to keep following Him right here on Earth. He wants you to *chase* Him. It's like He took off running after you said yes at the altar, and you have to run too if you want to catch up with Him. It's like when you were a child and you played tag. God came and showed you a quick glimpse of your future purpose and mission, and then He took off. He wants you to apprehend that for which you were apprehended. You can't catch Him if you stay there, sitting in your pew. You have to get up and cry out to Him. You have to develop big Mickey Mouse ears in your spirit so that you can hear Him even when what He says doesn't make a lot of sense to people.

When God says something, it *will* make enough sense to you. It made enough sense to Abraham. At seventy-five he said, "Pack the bags. I've got a thousand people looking to me for a paycheck and food, but you know what? We've moving, because I heard God!" (*What* God? Those people didn't know about the "God of Abraham" yet.) Abraham picked up and moved. Swallowing their objections, everybody else went with him.

He had the ability to believe what God said.

It's one thing to *hear* God. You also have to *believe* what you hear Him say. The Book of Hebrews talks about Abraham's ability to believe: "*By faith* Abraham obeyed when he was called to go out to the place which he would receive as an inheritance. And he went out, not knowing where he was going" (Heb. 11:8, NKJV, emphasis mine).

The Book of Hebrews also tells us that without faith it's impossible to please Him (Heb. 11:6). Abraham pleased God with his faith.

Abraham believed because he knew that God is always right. He knew that His mind does not run along the same tracks as our minds do. He already knew that it didn't make sense to question what God said, regardless of what his mind (or his wife's mind) told him.

It's a good idea to tell your mind to believe the next thing you hear from God. Tell yourself, "I'm going to start believing what I hear. I'm not going to back up. I'm not going to waver. I refuse to vacillate." Don't hem and haw and wait for another "sign" or another word of prophecy. Just believe what you hear Him say.

He had the ability to renounce security for the sake of God's mission.

Abraham was as comfortable and secure as a man could get in those days. He may have been more secure than a lot of us are. And yet he had the ability to make a divine denunciation of his present blessing in favor of the future promise.

If you are going to move into the purpose of God in your life, a time of divine denunciation will have to occur as well. A time will come when you too will have to remove yourself from the safe, predictable place, the place that you know is a sure thing, where you could keep on happily doing the same thing for the rest of your life. When that time comes, you'll have to believe that you really heard God and that He can be trusted to bring you into your promise.

You'll have to leave your lush valley in Ur, no matter how long you have lived there, and launch out in faith. You can have faith that God knows what He's doing because Abraham launched out in faith, and many others have done it too.

Jesus did it first when He left the glory of heaven to live on this earth. The Father's mission for His life involved leaving behind the security of heaven to sojourn on Earth for a while.

Peter launched out in faith when he and the other disciples were on that boat and Jesus came toward them, walking on the water. Eleven other men were right there, but only Peter took advantage of the opportunity and stepped out of the boat. (See Matthew 14.) The others were too scared to talk, even after Jesus said, "Don't be afraid; it is I." They were thinking, "Uh-uh! I'm not gettin' out of this boat!" But Peter said, "Lord, if that is You, bid me to come." (See verse 28.)

Granted, within a few minutes of starting to walk on the water, Peter began to sink. The same thing happens often when we step out on faith. That's not always a bad thing, because it teaches us to really depend on God, step after step. Regardless of the sinking times, I'd rather be a wet water walker than a dry boat talker!

He had the ability to stay focused on the mission.

Abram could have just changed his mind. He could have had second thoughts, especially after his wife began to wonder aloud what was going to become of them if they left Ur and went out into the howling wilderness.

But Abram stuck to it, and he kept on packing. He didn't worry about his advanced age or all of the other reasons he could have used to justify staying put.

He didn't change his mind once they set out, either. I suppose he could have. It's not as if he had lost the right to return. Nobody had driven him out of the land. But Abraham didn't change his mind, even after he found out that they really wouldn't be able to settle down at a new address anytime soon. Now, instead of having a settled lifestyle, they were nomadic. But Abraham had set his face to obey God, so he didn't let the challenges of his new lifestyle shake his decision.

Different kinds of problems came up all the time. Abraham could have decided it just wasn't worth it. Why on earth had God sent him on this wild-goose chase anyway? He hadn't told him *why*. God had just said *GO!*

He had the ability to accomplish the mission.

Because he had the ability to hear God and believe Him, and because he had the ability to renounce his security and stay focused on his mission, Abraham had the most important ability of all—he had the ability to *accomplish* the mission.

He had never done anything like this before. It took *years*. It involved additional missions. Abraham had to hear God, believe God, and obey God quite a few times in order to accomplish the mission of positioning himself for the future. He didn't wait until all his questions were answered. He took things as they came, one at a time. He kept his focus, even though he didn't always do everything perfectly (I always wondered about that time in Egypt when he claimed that his wife was his sister.)

The most important ability of all is the ability to accomplish the mission.

The main thing about Abraham was that he launched and he didn't turn back. I think God likes someone like that, someone who takes risks, even if they're foolish ones sometimes. If all the questions have to be answered before you step out and obey God, you'll never do anything.

That's probably why Jesus picked Peter to preach that powerful sermon on Pentecost. He knew he'd dare do it. Peter was the risk taker. (Faith is spelled R-I-S-K.) Peter was the one who had risked getting out of the boat. He was a loudmouth. He cut people's ears off.

I think that when Jesus was looking for the best candidate for preaching that sermon, he picked Peter because He knew that Peter would just launch. He would just walk out on the balcony and start to preach: "Hey, these men aren't drunk as you suppose. Here's what just happened..." (Acts 2). Peter had the ability to accomplish the mission. His ability came from his personality and his response to situations.

His ability to accomplish his mission also came from his *perseverance* and *creativity*. Peter just wouldn't quit. And with God's help, he always took the most difficult situation and converted it into something new and good.

Shake it off and step on it.

Those two words, *perseverance* and *creativity*, make me think of the story about the mule who fell down into a well.[2] When the farmer who owned the mule saw what had happened, he thought to himself, "I can't get him out. It's impossible." So, he decided to bury him. He took a shovel, and he started throwing dirt in on that poor mule.

And at first the mule was hysterical. "Oh, help, God! He's going to bury me alive!" But then the mule had a fantastic thought. The mule said to himself, "I'm just going to shake it off and step on it." And so as the farmer took shovel loads of dirt and threw it on that old mule, hour after hour after hour, that old mule would just shake it off and step on it, shake it off and step on it. After many hours, while the farmer kept shoveling the dirt in there, that donkey stepped out the top of it, triumphant.

Life will either bury you or bless you. It depends on what you do. Will you persevere? When they throw dirt on you, will you turn it into fertilizer and keep growing? When the dirt starts to rain down on you, shake it off, step on it, and go to higher ground.

Ready, Aim, Fire

You may remember how, when Elijah was about to be taken to heaven, Elisha asked for a double portion of his master's spirit, and he got it.

Elisha went on to do many exploits, and eventually he became an old man. This is where I want to pick up the story, because part of Elisha's "double-portion" mission was to speak into the life of the king of Israel about one of *his* missions, but the king's response wasn't bold enough to suit Elisha:

Elisha had become sick with the illness of which he would die. Then Joash the king of Israel came down to him, and wept over his face, and said, "O my father, my father, the chariots of Israel and their horsemen!" And Elisha said to him, "Take a bow and some arrows." So he took himself a bow and some arrows. Then he said to the king of Israel, "Put your hand on the bow." So he put his hand on it, and Elisha put his hands on the king's hands. And he said, "Open the east window"; and he opened it. Then Elisha said, "Shoot"; and he shot. And he said, "The arrow of the LORD's deliverance and the arrow of deliverance from Syria; for you must strike the Syrians at Aphek till you have destroyed them." Then he said, "Take the arrows"; so he took them. And he said to the king of Israel, "Strike the ground"; so he struck three times, and stopped. And the man of God was angry with him, and said, "You should have struck five or six times; then you would have struck Syria till you had destroyed it! But now you will strike Syria only three times."

—2 KINGS 13:14–19, NKJV

As a side note here, I want to point out that real victory is not won on the battlefield; it's won behind the scenes. Real victory is won in your private life, in your "bed chamber," if you will. Real victory is won in your inner man first, and then you will see evidence on the battlefield.

So Elisha had King Joash with him in his bedchamber, and he said to King Joash, "Take a bow and arrows." He took them privately. It's like when we take up our weapons of prayer every morning in private. What we do with them is important. Our public success or failure reflects what happens in our private life. The two always coordinate with each other; the public manifests the private.

194

Elisha had the king pick up his weapon, even though he was just in Elisha's private room and not out on the battlefield, fighting against Syria. (Some Bible translations say "Aram.") In the same way, God will have us pick up our weapons in our private prayer times. There's nobody watching. It's just you and God. That's where the real business gets transacted. That's where you really *pick up* your weapons, because there's no point in faking it anyway. It doesn't matter if you're not much of a warrior.

Joash was the old king, and he was losing on the battlefield. Elisha was an old man, and he was a prophet; he'd never been a warrior. But they could both obey the word of the Lord if they wanted to.

The king picked up his bow and arrow, and he shot once out the window, as Elisha said. So far, so good. The devil would have preferred to have him shrug it off as foolishness and stay inside, feeling helpless and hopeless. But Joash had done what Elisha told him to do—he opened up his eyes and focused them outside the open window, and then he shot an arrow out there.

It's the same with us, except our "arrows" are our words. Our arrows are our confession, and our worship and our prayers. We need to let them fly out of us. We need to send our words out in the direction we want them to go. In other words, we need to start talking victory when we're staring at defeat. We need to start talking healing when we're feeling sick. We need to start talking blessing and prosperity when we don't have anything. We need to talk about living when we feel like dying. We need to speak about marching when we feel like quitting. That's how we shoot our word arrows.

Sometimes you just have to say, "I'm going to shoot my way out!" Nobody can do it for you—not your preacher or your spouse.

Elisha didn't shoot the arrows for the king. He told him what to do, but the king had to do it himself.

After the king shot one arrow, Elisha told him to take the rest of the arrows and start striking the ground with them. This didn't make any more sense than shooting an arrow out of the open window, but King Joash did it. He hit the ground with the arrows hard three times. There! That ought to show those Syrians!

But Elisha was furious. For an old guy, he could still get mad. He said, "Why did you stop?" Because if he had kept hitting the ground even a couple more times, he would have been assured of complete victory over his enemies. But he stopped short of that. Now he would win some battles, but he wouldn't win the war.

Before we are too quick to judge the king, we need to think about our way of doing things. Don't we do that ourselves sometimes? We stop just short of God's best. We think that three times is good enough. It doesn't seem like anything is happening, so we quit. Maybe God told you, "Keep preaching and preaching and preaching, Sunday after Sunday and week after week," but your congregation stays small, and nobody seems to get anything out of your preaching. Nothing seems to improve, so you slack off.

The devil has your number.

Don't slack off. You need to keep doing what God told you to do. And you need to do it with some *intensity*! Sometimes when you are on the verge of a breakthrough, it's even more important to keep going. Too many people give up when they're right on the verge of a breakthrough. That can be the most discouraging time of all.

Instead of turning back, you need to say to yourself, "I'm too close to back up now." You need to realize that the devil has your number. You need to recognize how he works against you. It's like the devil called a board meeting and said to all his chief demons, "What is our greatest weapon against this person?" Some demons suggested lust or greed or the usual things. And then one of them said, "Our greatest weapon against the believer is discouragement." And that's what he uses to make you quit, especially right before you're about to run through the finish line.

Next time you feel discouraged, don't quit. All it means is that the devil is so desperate to stop you that he has sent his most powerful weapon against you. You should stand up and start praising God for the discouragement. Say, "Thank You, Jesus! Thank You, God! I must be really bothering the devil, and I must be getting real close to something—because I'm so discouraged!"

The devil doesn't know what to do with a child of God who talks like that. You just took hold of the very thing he tried to mess you up with, and you turned it around. You just got encouraged about your discouragement!

Don't Let Your Dream Die

Now, there's one more wonderful detail in this story of King Joash and Elisha. It's not about the military outcome, which worked out just as it was predicted by the arrows. It's about Elisha himself, who had been faithfully pursuing his dream full steam ahead, all his life, and who had just taken time out to help the king.

The end of his life came soon after he helped Joash. He was sick already when he helped him. Soon, he died.

I wonder if Elisha realized that he hadn't quite hit the "double portion" mark yet. If you count the major miracles that his master Elijah had performed and then you count the number that Elisha did, you'll see that Elijah performed seven major miracles before he was taken up to heaven. Then Elisha put on his mantle, and he began to perform miracles. He hit seven, and he kept performing miracles. He hit eight, nine, ten, even eleven and twelve. He had gotten up to thirteen when he died.

He was on his deathbed, one miracle short of two times seven, or a double portion. A double portion had been God's promise to him. Having a "double portion" of Elijah's miracle-working spirit was Elisha's God-given dream. You have to wonder—maybe he could have squeezed in another miracle if he hadn't taken time to help Joash. In a way, Elisha had died helping somebody else reach their dream of victory.

The same kind of thing can happen with you when you choose to give from your deficit. You encourage somebody even when you're discouraged yourself. You almost feel like a hypocrite because things aren't that great in your life right now, but you do it. You pray for somebody's healing, even though you're sick yourself, or you give somebody your last dime, knowing all the time you have financial needs pressing on you. Let me tell you a sure way to get discouraged. Just get in a room and think about nothing but yourself, and you'll be discouraged in no time flat.

When you reach out to somebody else, it's good for you. You get your focus off yourself, God takes pleasure in you, and your discouragement is dispelled.

A sure way to get discouraged is to think about nothing but yourself.

So, it's as if Elisha died having given his last miracle to somebody else. People took Elisha's body, and they put it in a grave. (I can see them starting to chisel into a headstone, "He almost got the double portion.") Soon afterward, some people came to bury another dead man in the same cemetery. Just then, a Moabite raid rolled through. They had to get rid of the body in a hurry, so they put it in on top of Elisha's body in his sepulchre.

Then look what happened:

> Then Elisha died, and they buried him. And the raiding bands from Moab invaded the land in the spring of the year. So it was, as they were burying a man, that suddenly they spied a band of raiders; and they put the man in the tomb of Elisha; and when the man was let down and touched the bones of Elisha, he revived and stood on his feet.
>
> —2 KINGS 13:20–21, NKJV

Elisha didn't revive, but the *other* dead man did. What must the formerly dead man have thought when he found himself walking on his own two feet all of a sudden? I bet those grave diggers came out of there in a hurry too!

When that dead body hit the bones of Elisha, it was miracle number fourteen! Double portion!

The devil may have thought he managed to rob Elisha of the full double portion, but he didn't after all. God got the last laugh. He was true to His word. Elisha did get a complete double portion of Elijah's seven miracles, even though his fourteenth and last miracle happened after he was in his grave!

God was faithful. Elisha's dream did not die with him. That's the kind of God we serve, every one of us.

Anointed dreams

In the story of Jacob and his dream of the ladder of angels, Jacob woke up, and he said, "Surely the LORD is in this place; and I knew it not" (Gen. 28:16). He had been running from his enemies, and then God had blessed him. He had started to see his life with new eyes, and he knew that God would preserve Him because He had a future for him.

So what did he do? He took some oil, and he anointed the rock he had been using for a pillow. His dream had happened while his head was on that rock. He wanted to transform that place of hardship into a memorial of God's absolute faithfulness. God had spoken to him there. He had promised him that piece of land for posterity. He also promised that he would have *countless* descendants and that "all the families of the earth" would be blessed through them (Gen. 28:13–15).

Jacob's dream was a little bit like Elisha's double portion. In the lives of both Jacob and Elisha, *God* would be the One who would get the most glory, because His faithfulness would outlive their earthly lives. It would spill over into the lives of their descendants like anointing oil.

Jacob anointed the place of his dream as a testimony to God's utter faithfulness. And then he proceeded to live every day of his life in the light of that knowledge. We can do the same thing. Much of the fulfillment of Jacob's dream from God happened after he was gone too.

What dream has God given you? What *new* dream has He added to the old ones? Whether you're just starting out or building on past dreams, what has God told you that He wants to do with you?

Whatever it is, God is true to His word, and God's Word is true. God is faithful. He will have you walking in the purpose of your dream if you say yes to Him. Say yes, and then do something to keep remembering where you're going. Above all, keep remembering how faithful God is. He keeps making your dream happen right up to, and past, the day of your physical death. Our faithful God is worthy of every word of praise we can ever proclaim!

REVIEW

Never Too Old

- Because you're *here*, you can be sure that God has a plan and purpose for your life, whether you're old or young.

- Abraham packed up his wife and the whole company of his dependents and set out on a nomadic life. The only reason he would do this was because of these important characteristics. He had:

    - The ability to hear God

    - The ability to believe what God said

    - The ability to denounce security for the sake of God's mission

- ◎ The ability to stay focused on the mission

- ◎ The ability to accomplish the mission

◎ Abraham was a risk taker. So was Elisha. So was Peter. Are you a risk taker?

◎ God will always be faithful to His word. God is so faithful, He will keep fulfilling His word even after you die, which is what He did for Elisha and also for Jacob.

Chapter 12

PUT AWAY YOUR
MEASURING STICK

T HE NAME OF THIS BOOK IS *BELIEVE*

That You Can. Can you believe that you

can? Can you believe the message of this book for your

own life? Do you believe that you can reach your highest

potential? Can you believe that all things are possible—for *you*—with your all-powerful God?

After all these chapters, I hope that you have not only been able to identify God's dream for your life, but also that you are now *living* it, right this minute. If you find that you have even the slightest hesitation about this, stop right here and put this book down long enough to speak life to your dream.

Say to your dream, "Dream, *live*! In the name of Jesus, come fully alive and step out of your grave clothes. Dream, I call you out of the shadows. It's not time for you to die or sleep, because God is alive and *I'm* still alive. I tell you to live, dream, live. Live!"

You can't create your own dream or choose your own dream, because it comes from God, and He is the One who needs to give it to you. But you can choose to let it live and thrive. You can decide to pick it up and run with it. You can purposely take hold of your destiny.

You can't choose who your momma or your daddy are. You can't choose how you came into this world. But you can choose to be blessed. You can say yes to God's plan for your life. You were created for a purpose, and God wants you to walk in it.

When your Creator God made you and put you in your mother's womb, He took everything that you now consider negative about yourself, and He factored it in. He took everything that you now consider positive about yourself, and He factored that in too. He put it all into His computer, so to speak, and He hit a button, and out came something called your "high calling" (Phil. 3:14). Out came the wonderful plan God has for your life. He locked it up inside you, and He made two keys—one for you and one for Himself.

You were created for a purpose,
and God wants you to walk in it.

Then He put you into an environment that reaches into the deepest places in your soul and spirit. As you grow up and start to wake up the thing for which you were called, you pick up your key. Since one key by itself isn't enough, you start to look around for another one. You're pretty sure that God must have it, and you become determined to catch up with Him.

The more you pursue Him, the closer you get; you really do, although sometimes it feels like a divine hide-and-seek game. God wants to be found. He won't make it too hard for you. When it's time for your destiny to come to light, it will. The thrill of discovery is only going to be overshadowed by the thrill of fulfillment when you have finished the rest of the race of your life. The satisfaction you feel is always increased by the fact that you have had to work for something. You have to press in, always following His quiet voice.

In any case, it's never too late. God's timing is perfect. He's never late, not even by one millisecond. Believe He can show you your dream, and believe He can carry you through to its completion. Believe that *you* can follow Him on that long way ahead. You can!

God Knows What He's Doing

Put your faith in the right place. Put it in God. He is the One who knows what He's doing. Don't put your faith in somebody else. The rest of us can only point the way to Him after we put our faith in Him.

You may look at your life right now and say, "Jentezen, I don't see much evidence of what you're talking about. I've been paying attention, but I still don't see it. I still have the same problems. I just cannot see the blessing in it."

Well, I'd just say to you what I've been saying throughout this book: Keep going. You are not the exception in God's kingdom. He doesn't have any exceptions in His kingdom. God knows what He's doing with you. And He loves you. Your life right now may be in a time of "small beginnings." Remember that line in the Bible about not despising small beginnings? (See Zechariah 4:10.)

I read somewhere that when the Coca-Cola Company started in Atlanta, they sold four hundred bottles of Coke in their first year. (Today, I have people in my church who drink that many Cokes a year all by themselves!) If I had been the president of the Coca-Cola Company, I might have quit after a slow start like that. But they didn't quit. They kept going, and they kept gathering speed. Now, everywhere I travel around the world, South America, Europe, you name it, I see signs for Coca-Cola. In 2007, they sold 22.7 billion units of Coke.[1] It's a good thing they didn't despise their small beginnings.

Good thing Simon Peter didn't drop the ball every time the Lord passed it to him, even though he did drop it sometimes. If he had doubted his vision or wavered in his faith, millions of souls for generations would have been affected. God knew what He was doing when He picked Simon Peter and when He put him through the things he had to see and do and say. Peter said yes to God, and now the rest is history—such important events that they were recorded for us in the New Testament itself. He didn't let go of his assignment, even in the face of the hardships or his mistakes.

God knows what He's doing—all the time. He doesn't go take

a nap and miss something. He is faithful, and He will always do what He said He would do. Whether He has you in a wilderness time, a time of sowing, or a time of harvest, He's with you. He's the One who has the key to your heart and to your future.

As time goes on, you will realize that your burden has become your passion.

When it's time for something to happen, He'll make sure it happens, whether it's as slow as a spring thaw or as fast as a woman having a baby in the backseat of a taxicab. When it's time, it's time—time for your vision to be unlocked and for you to embrace it. God has a plan for you, and it's already in action right now.

He who runs may read it.

Let's retrace the steps of your vision, remembering what we first talked about in chapter 1, where I quoted this particular passage that so well sums up how your dreams and visions from God operate:

> Then the LORD answered me and said:
> "Write the vision
> And make it plain on tablets,
> That he may run who reads it.
> For the vision is yet for an appointed time;
> But at the end it will speak, and it will not lie.
> Though it tarries, wait for it;
> Because it will surely come,

It will not tarry....

The just shall live by his faith."

—HABAKKUK 2:2–4, NKJV

Habakkuk shows us that your vision will begin with a burden in your spirit, something that will feel like a weight. As time goes on, it will get clearer and clearer to you. You will realize that your burden has become your passion. After a while, instead of carrying it around like a burden, it may begin to almost carry you.

However, that doesn't mean that the journey is going to be smooth. You will face hindrances and obstacles and all kinds of hassles. Your character will be shaped and formed in the process, and you will grow in your faith. One of the ways you will know that you have taken hold of the right vision is that it will be bigger than you are. It will still be on your screen even when your life feels like World War III.

Just focus on it, and focus on the Lord who gave it to you. You will have to take every step by faith. Faith steps are the only kinds of steps that will get you anywhere. Keep your eyes on Him and on the dream He has given you, and "walk in the steps of that faith of our father Abraham" (Rom. 4:12).

Another way you will know that you have taken hold of the right vision is that it will be connected in some way with the love of God and the harvest of the kingdom. It may be a small-seeming thing. Not everybody can be called to preach to stadiums full of people. Your job may be behind the scenes. It may seem very ordinary. But if it has God's seal of approval, it will be special.

Last but not least, it's a good idea to take Habakkuk's advice—write down your vision. Then, when life gets hectic, you won't lose track of it. When you hit a fork in the road, you'll know which way to turn. And when you need to draw on your patience and even your perseverance, you will have something to refer to.

Old Habakkuk knew what he was talking about. He had first-hand experience. Praise God, he wrote down his wise exhortation so that we can still read it today.

Your God will not let you down. He can't. It would go against His character to let you down. Believe that you can because you believe that *He* can. You *can* depend on Him!

Put Away Your Measuring Stick

Wherever you find yourself in the process, don't put limits on what God can do! He is infinite, and so are the possibilities for the dreams that He gives people. The trouble is, we have a very strong tendency to put limits on Him, especially when it comes to our dreams and visions for our lives. We think we are the final authority on our lives and that we know what's best and what's realistic.

Believe that you can because you believe that He can. You can depend on Him!

Be careful that you don't end up trying to stand against God just because you think you know what you're doing. God Himself doesn't want you to keep measuring yourself or your circumstances against your idea of reality. How do I know that? Because He put what He thinks about "measuring" in the Bible: "I lifted up mine eyes again, and looked, and behold a man with a measuring line in his hand....And, behold, the angel that talked with me went forth, and another angel went out to meet him" (Zech. 2:1, 3).

See the picture in your mind. There was a young man who took a measuring line because he was going to try to measure what God was doing in the city of Jerusalem. *God was disturbed by that.* He was disturbed enough to dispatch an angel from heaven on the spot to stop him. And when the angel said to the young man, "Son, what are you doing?" and the man said that he was going to measure the width, breadth, and height of Jerusalem to see what God was doing in the earth, the angel said back to him, "Put your measuring line away, son, because anything that God is involved in is *unmeasurable.*"

God didn't want anybody to put limits on what He could or would do. God knew that as soon as people started measuring the city, they would define the boundaries. They would tend to set boundaries, and they would box God in. Their measurements would make a statement about what they felt God is capable of.

In the context of a book about finding and following God's vision for your life, this idea of measuring lines has a lot of application, because, instead of believing that we can accomplish what God gives us to do (even if it seems impossible), we put limits on everything. In theory, we may believe that God can accomplish the impossible, but in practice, we draw boundaries.

God says, "I'm going to use you," and your first response is, "But I come from the bad side of town. I don't have any education. My daddy left my family when I was a kid. I've got so many handicaps..."

Don't you think your response should be more like Mary's response? The angel told her that she would become pregnant even though she was a virgin and that she would bear the Son of God.

She was startled, but she didn't object to the word. Her response was, "How shall this be?...Behold the handmaid of the Lord; be it unto me according to thy word" (Luke 1:34, 38). No ifs, ands, or buts. She didn't put any limits on her unlimited God.

Pharisee measuring sticks

It's as if we have a "Pharisee spirit" in us. I say that because in Jesus's day, the Pharisees were the professional "measurers."

God may say to you, "I've anointed your son to serve Me in a special way." But immediately you take your measuring line and hold it up against your son and read the markings on it. It doesn't have markings in inches. Instead, the markings read things like, "learning disorder," "not college material," and "not interested in God." So we measure him and find him deficient—in *our* estimation. As a result, we throw out the word of the Lord without even really considering it.

The Pharisee spirit likes to hang around churches. It likes to pull out the religious tape measure and walk around measuring people, saying, "Hmmm, hmmm. That's a nice suit of clothes. But you used to be a drug addict, didn't you? You've got a little past, don't you? I heard that you're divorced. I won't expect much from you."

I know you've done that kind of thing, because I've done it myself. We've all done it, and we've all had it done to us, sometimes even in the name of "humility." When the angel came to Gideon and said, "The LORD is with you, you mighty man of valor!" (Judg. 6:12), Gideon had his measuring line ready to use on that statement.

His response was practically instantaneous: "I am the least in my father's house..." (Judg. 6:15). So what? How is that relevant?

When God calls you to do something, and especially when He sends His personal angelic emissary, I don't think He needs to consult with your family first. It didn't matter one bit what Gideon's family or clan status was. If God's angel had just stepped onto the threshing floor to make an announcement, it was time for Gideon to say, "Well then, just show me what you want me to do."

The only concept of measurement you need is one of God's infinite ability and capability. God's call will supersede everything else in your life. He is unmeasurable and so is everything He does.

Unlimited supply

Some of you have looked at your bills recently. Maybe you just did it again last night. And then you looked at your paycheck, and it's not enough to pay them. Out came your old measuring tape, and you said, as the disciples said before the Lord multiplied a few loaves and fish to feed five thousand–plus people, "What are they among so many?" (John 6:9). One of the disciples even said, "If we had two hundred pennies worth of bread, it would only be enough for a few of them, and we don't even have that much." (See Mark 6:37; John 6:7.) Your version is, "See, what is so little income with so many bills? Even if I had two jobs, it wouldn't be enough."

The only concept of measurement you need is one of God's infinite ability and capability.

That's a tape-measure mentality in action. Over against our limited version of the possibilities, we have God. God has a "maximum mentality." You need to stop applying your minimum mentality with your maximum God. You need to stop measuring your earning capacity by what you earned last year or by your previous achievements in the working world. That just puts a cap on what God can do.

He is a God of increase. He is a God of abundance. With Him, if we will only give Him what we have and trust Him with it, and begin to obey Him when He tells us what to do, we will start to see increase. Get rid of that measuring tape. Sell it on eBay or something. Get it out of your house!

Don't measure yourself out of a miracle.

Don't let yourself get influenced by the people around you who say, "God might be strong enough to do anything, but I don't think He's doing those kinds of things today. He used to heal. He used to deliver. He used to provide supernaturally. He used to call people. But don't hold your breath these days. It's kind of outdated to think that He'll do things like that."

Don't hinder the miraculous from happening in your life. Don't be like the Israelites who should have known better because they had experienced so many miracles, but they went ahead and said, "Can God furnish a table in the wilderness?" (Ps. 78:19).

Sure, they didn't have any food in sight. Out there in the wilderness, they didn't have any restaurants, not even fast food. There were no convenience stores for five hundred miles. And they were genuinely worried about starving to death. But that shouldn't have made them conclude that God was too limited to help them. God could—and did—provide for them. He was bigger than famine and thirst then, and He still is today.

Or if you bring it up to Jesus's time, let's look at the people who lived in Nazareth, Jesus's hometown. The Gospels tell us that when Jesus came into His home city, He couldn't make any headway against the "measuring lines" of the townspeople:

> And when he was come into his own country, he taught them in their synagogue, insomuch that they were astonished, and said, Whence hath this man this wisdom, and these mighty works? Is not this the carpenter's son? is not his mother called Mary? and his brethren, James, and Joses, and Simon, and Judas? And his sisters, are they not all with us? Whence then hath this man all these things? And they were offended in him. But Jesus said unto them, A prophet is not without honour, save in his own country, and in his own house. And he did not many mighty works there because of their unbelief.
>
> —MATTHEW 13:54–58

The townspeople just looked at the evidence. Hadn't their kids grown up alongside Jesus when He was a boy? Wasn't He the one whose mother, Mary, got pregnant with Him before she was married? Not only was He illegitimate, but now He was also going around eating with sinners and drunks. He had a bunch of dusty people following Him around, including some harlots. Obviously, He was just an ordinary Nazarene, except for being a little peculiar. And those townspeople talked themselves out of their miracles—miracles they really needed—without half trying.

What did Jesus do? He just shoved along to the next town, and the next. Everywhere *else* He went, the Bible says He healed them all. (See, for example, Matthew 4:24; 12:15; Luke 4:40; 6:19.) Clearly, the low faith He found in Nazareth had something to do with the low level of miracles there. The people's measuring lines cut their faith down to the point that it was not big enough anymore.

Much more than ankle deep

We can find another "measuring line" in the Book of Ezekiel:

> In the twenty-fifth year of our captivity, at the beginning of the year, on the tenth day of the month, in the fourteenth year after the city was captured, on the very same day the hand of the LORD was upon me; and He took me there. In the visions of God He took me into the land of Israel and set me on a very high mountain; on it toward the south was something like the structure of a city. He took me there, and behold, there was a man whose appearance was like the appearance of bronze. *He had a line of flax and a measuring rod in his hand, and he stood in the gateway.*
>
> —EZEKIEL 40:1–3, NKJV, EMPHASIS MINE

The man (or angel) took Ezekiel on a complete tour of the temple and its courtyards, measuring everything in sight with his measuring rod. Then, when they came to the eastern gate, where water was gushing out and flowing down away from the temple, they waded in, and the man began to measure the depth of the water:

> And when the man that had the line in his hand went forth eastward, he measured a thousand cubits, and he brought me through the waters; the waters were to the ancles. Again he measured a thousand, and brought me through the waters; the waters were to the knees. Again he measured a thousand, and

215

brought me through; the waters were to the loins. Afterward he measured a thousand; and it was a river that I could not pass over: for the waters were risen, waters to swim in, a river that could not be passed over.

—EZEKIEL 47:3–5

Notice that as long as they kept measuring, they could only get ankle deep, knee deep, and waist deep. After they waded in up to their waists, it got too deep to walk in; it was a river. They couldn't measure the river. It was deep and wide, and its banks were lush with fruit trees. That river was unlimited, full of life and blessing.

If you accept your own assigned playing field, nobody can limit your success.

That's a picture of our life in the Lord—unlimited in blessing, unmeasurable. If you put away your measuring lines, tapes, and rods and just let the Son of God show you where He wants you to go, you will soon forget about boundaries and limits.

The potential of your dream is tremendous. If you accept your own assigned playing field, nobody can limit your success. God is the One who decides how "successful" you will be, because no matter who plants and sows and tills the soil, it is God who gives the increase (1 Cor. 3:7). You can't make your own seed grow any more than you can make the sun shine. Your life is in His hands.

Unlimited!

Once you've had increase in your life, you will be able to recognize that it wasn't your brilliance that did it. It was God's doing. He could have left you back in your field as a sower. All your life you could have kept sowing and resowing the seed. But He gave the increase, and now you can see the whole picture.

Let your dream live, and let it flow! You can flow with it. God wants you to grab hold of your dream so that at the end of your life on Earth, you can say with the apostle Paul, "I was not disobedient unto the heavenly vision" (Acts 26:19). Put away your measuring line, and let God take you to meet your destiny.

Believe that you can! "For with God nothing shall be impossible" (Luke 1:37)!

REVIEW

Put Away Your Measuring Stick

- Say to your dream, "Dream, *live*! God is alive, and I'm still alive, and I call you out of the shadows. Dream, live!"

- God knows what He's doing. When it's time for something to happen, He'll make sure it happens, whether it happens slow or fast.

- The stages of the development of your dream from God will include these: (1) A burden grows in your heart and develops into a passion. (2) Your dream will be big enough to overcome all the hindrances that come against you. (3) You will keep your focus on your dream and on the God who gave it to you, walking in faith every step of the journey. (4) If you persevere, you will overcome all obstacles, and your dream will become a reality.

⊙ Put away your measuring stick. There is absolutely no limit to what your God can do!

Prayer

Father,

In Jesus's name I pray for Your passion to be ignited in me so that Your vision and dream for my life will become clear to me so that I can follow it. I desire to find my appointed place in Your kingdom harvest.

What is the dream that You have appointed for my life? I want to find and fulfill the destiny for which You created me.

I want to trust in You with complete faith so that I can break through every limitation into victory.

Give me the faith to believe that I can!

Amen.

Notes

Six
Making Assets of Your Liabilities

1. Chickfila.com, "Company Fact Sheet," http://chickfila.com/#facts (accessed July 21, 2008).

2. "Richest Americans," *Forbes*, #380, S. Truett Cathy, www.forbes .com/lists/2007/54/richlist07_S-Truett-Cathy_AARY.html.

3. Truett Cathy, *Eat More Chikin: Inspire More People* (n.p.: Looking Glass Books, 2002).

Seven
Living in the Faith Zone

1. From biography of Tom Monaghan on American Dreams: Books, Speakers, and Events, http://www.usdreams.com/Monaghan7677.html (accessed July 9, 2008).

2. Answers.com, "Biography: Tom Monaghan," http://www.answers .com/topic/tom_monaghan (accessed July 21, 2008).

3. Peter J. Boyer, "The Deliverer," *The New Yorker*, February 19, 2007, 88. Abstract at http://www.newyorker.com/reporting/2007/02/19/070219fa_ fact_boyer (accessed July 9, 2008).

Nine
Keep Climbing

1. Wolfgang Saxon, "Joseph Fowler, 99, Builder of Warships and Disney's Parks," New York Times, December 14, 1993, http://query.nytimes .com/gst/fullpage.html?res=9F0CE1DC1030F937A25751C1A965958260& scp=4&sq=Joseph%20Fowler&st=cse (accessed July 21, 2008).

2. Disney Legends, "Joe Fowler," www.legends.disney.go.com/legends/ detail?key=Joe+Fowler (accessed July 21, 2008).

Eleven
Never Too Old

1. "In the Garden" by C. Austin Miles. Public Domain.

2. Retold from *Discovering Your Destiny*, by Bob Gass (Gainesville, FL: Bridge-Logos Publishers, 2001), 65.

Twelve
Put Away Your Measuring Stick

1. The Coca-Cola Company, "Financial Overview," http//www.thecoca -colacompany.com/ourcompany/ar/financialoverview.html (accessed July 21, 2008).

To find out more about
Jentezen Franklin Ministries,
visit us online at:

www.freechapel.org

www.jentezenfranklin.org

www.fastingmovement.org

www.forwardconference.org

Open the door to a deeper, more intimate, more powerful relationship with God

In one of the best available books on the topic, Franklin explains the spiritual power of fasting and offers a deeper understanding of the benefits available to all who participate. Discover everything you need to know to unlock the power of biblical fasting, including:

- The types of fasts described in the Bible and how to choose the right one
- The connection between fasting and prayer
- What to expect physically, mentally, and spiritually
- And more!

ISBN: 978-1-59979-258-3
$15.99